NEW WEB RESOURCE
FROM THE NATIONAL RESOURCE CENTER FOR HEALTH AND SAFETY IN CHILD CARE AND EARLY EDUCATION
www.healthykids.us

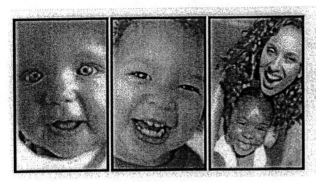 

Healthy Kids, Healthy Care

Written for **Parents** on Topics they want to know about!

Based on **Caring for Our Children: National Health and Safety Performance Standards: Guidelines for Out-of-Home Child Care, 2ⁿᵈ Ed**

34 Topics covered:

Allergies, Asthma and other Chronic Illnesses
Background checks
Biting and Other Aggressive Behaviors
Caregiver Health
Caregiver Qualifications and Training
Child Abuse
Child Care Health Consultants

Child: Staff Ratios
Children with Special Needs
Cleaning and Sanitizing Practices
Complaints
Dental health
Diapering
Discipline
Emergency Preparedness
First Aid and CPR
Food Preparation

Handwashing
Immunization
Injury Prevention
Meals and Snacks
Medicine in Child Care
Physical Fitness and Healthy Weight
Playground Safety
Respecting Differences
Selecting Child Care

Sick Children
SIDS Risk Reduction
Source of Health and Dental Care
Supervision
Toilet Training
Toxic Substances
Toys
Transportation

Material Presented in Tabbed Sections
Key Questions
Want to Know More
How to Help Your Caregiver
Additional Resources
****

Coming Soon!!

Healthy Kids, Healthy Care will soon be available in *Spanish* on the Web.
English and Spanish Print Copies will also be available for Purchase.

Check the National Resource Center for Health and Safety in Child Care and Early Education Website
http://nrc.uchsc.edu for updates

Guía de Pasos Principales para el Cuidado de Nuestros Niños, 2nda Edición

(Stepping Stones to Using Caring for Our Children, 2nd Edition)

Guía de Pasos Principales para el Cuidado de Nuestros Niños (Stepping Stones to Using Caring for Our Children) is a valuable tool for child care providers, health consultants and professionals, and families to identify key health and safety practices that have the greatest impact on disease, disability and death (morbidity and mortality) in out-of-home child care.

Guía de Pasos Principales contains 233 standards selected as a subset of the 659 national health and safety performance standards in *Caring For Our Children: National Health and Safety Performance Standard: Guidelines for Out- of-Home Child Care Programs, 2nd Edition* (CFOC), developed by the American Academy of Pediatrics, the American Public Health Association and the National Resource Center for Health and Safety in Child Care and Early Education .

Chapters include the following topic areas:
- ❖ **Staffing**
- ❖ **Program: Activities for Healthy Development**
- ❖ **Health Protection and Health Promotion**
- ❖ **Nutrition and Food Service**
- ❖ **Facilities, Supplies, Equipment and Transportation**
- ❖ **Infectious Diseases**
- ❖ **Children who are Eligible for Services Under IDEA**
- ❖ **Administration.**

Guía de Pasos Principales para el Cuidado de Nuestros Niños is available:
Online full text at http://nrc.uchsc.edu/STEPPING/SteppingStonesSpanish.pdf
and
For **purchase** from:
UCHSC Bookstore
4200 E. 9th Ave, Mail Stop A057
Denver, CO 80262
Phone: 1-800-591-2884
Email: Kristin.Sponsler@uchsc.edu or
Dirk.Stricker@uchsc.edu
ENGLISH OR SPANISH
Price: $6.00 per copy plus shipping

National Resource Center for Health and Safety in Child Care and Early Education

The Directory of Critical Information for Helping Children

Compiled and Edited by

Natalie Ireland, LSW
Tanya Freeman
Hennie Shore

The Center for Applied Psychology, Inc.
King of Prussia, Pennsylvania

The Directory of Critical Information for Helping Children
Compiled and Edited by: Natalie Ireland, LSW, Tanya Freeman and Hennie Shore

Published by:
The Center for Applied Psychology, Inc.
P.O. Box 61587
King of Prussia, PA 19406 U.S.A.
(800) 962-1141

The Center for Applied Psychology, Inc. is the publisher of Childswork/Childsplay, a catalog of products for mental health professionals, teachers, and parents who wish to help children with their developmental, social and emotional growth.

Printed in the United States of America.

ISBN 1-882732-59-6

Table of Contents

Table of Contents

The Directory of Critical Information for Helping Children was compiled from a range of resources and directories. It is designed to be the source to which you will turn first for answers whenever you need to find information and resources on childhood problems and disorders.

The first section highlights General Information and Advocacy Groups that focus on a specific disorder, as well as hotlines, self-help groups, and on-line information to give you a broad spectrum of resources from which to choose. The section devoted to Clearinghouses provides resource sources that collect and disseminate information related to the mental health of children. The Model Treatment Programs listed in this Directory were selected from the National Mental Health Association's *Directory of Model Programs to Prevent Mental Health Disorders*. Others were selected from the psychological literature.

Sections listing General Mental Health Organizations, Professional Mental Health Associations, Organizations for Mental Health Issues Affecting Minorities, and State Mental Health Organizations also are included, as are synopses of Federal Laws Pertaining to the Rights of Special Needs Children. Finally, the Product Sources section lists organizations that publish and/or sell books, games, videotapes, audiotapes, computer software and other items for helping children with their mental health needs.

We have attempted to assemble the most current and important information available on sources and treatment programs that focus on the mental health of children and their families. However, in a directory of this scope, there invariably will be omissions. If you feel that an entry should be added to any of the listings within this book, or if an error needs to be corrected, please take a moment to fill out the form at the back of the Directory and we will consider adding it to the next edition.

This resource is just the first step toward helping children. The organizations and people listed within will provide the data and services you need to help the children with whom you work. The information is listed alphabetically within each section. It is our hope that this resource will serve as a catalyst in your search for information, and that it will make your job a little easier.

ADOPTED CHILDREN

It is estimated that two percent of the U.S. population are adopted people. Recent surveys indicate that 8 to 10 percent of outpatient child and adolescent mental health visits and up to 20 percent of inpatient bed utilization in inpatient child and adolescent psychiatric units and residential treatment centers involve young people who have been adopted.

—from "Adopted Children at School" by S. Erbaugh in *Helping Children Grow Up in the '90s*, National Association of School Psychologists, 1992.

General Information/Advocacy Groups

Child Welfare League of America
440 First St. NW, Suite 310
Washington, DC 20001-2085
(202) 638-2952
(202) 638-4004 (Fax)
National consortium of numerous organizations offers information, support, and referrals related to abused and neglected children and their families, family preservation, child care, foster care, adoption, residential group homes, teens who are parents or pregnant. Child Welfare League offers a wide array of publications on these issues.

Council for the Equal Rights in Adoption
401 E. 74th St., Suite 17D
New York, NY 10022
(212) 988-0110
Nonprofit organization seeks equal rights for those involved in adoption and the preservation of families. Has newsletter entitled: *ACCESS*.

Learning and Behavior
Minneapolis Children's Medical Center
2525 Chicago Ave. South
Minneapolis, MN 55404
(612) 813-6354
Distributes a packet of materials of interest to parents, school personnel, and others concerned with the special needs of adoptive families and children.

National Adoption Information Clearinghouse
11426 Rockville Pike, Suite 410
Rockville, MD 20852
(301) 231-6512

National Institute of Mental Health (NIMH)
5600 Fishers Lane, Room 7C-02
Rockville, MD 20857
(301) 443-4513
Complete resource of information and up-to-date research.

National Resource Center for Special Needs Adoption
16205 Northland Dr., Suite 120
Southfield, MI 48075
(810) 443-7080
Provides a forum for adoption practitioners, policymakers, and advocates to contribute and share their knowledge and expertise. The purpose of the center is to improve the effectiveness and quality of adoption and postadoption services nationwide for children with special needs. The center serves as a resource for organizations and professionals through consultation, technical assistance, training, and a variety of written and videotaped materials. A publication list and information packet are available.

Partners for Adoption
4527 Montgomery Dr., Suite A
P.O. Box 2791
Santa Rosa, CA 95405
(707) 539-9068
Nonprofit organization's goal is to promote the placement of every child into a permanent, nurturing family.

Resources for Adoptive Parents
4049 Brookside Ave. South
Minneapolis, MN 55416
(612) 926-6959

Hotlines/Helplines

Concerned United Birthparents
(800) 822-2777

Gladney Center
(800) GLADNEY

National Adoption Center
(800) TO-ADOPT

Self-Help/Support Groups

Adoptee's Liberty Movement Association (ALMA)
P.O. Box 727, Radio City Station
New York, NY 10101-0727
(212) 581-1568
Founded in 1971 to connect adoptees with one another to exchange views on the adoptive situation and for mutual assistance in the search for natural parents. The ALMA International Reunion Registry Database is a multilevel, computerized cross-indexing system containing the vital statistics of adoptees, natural parents, and all parents separated by adoption for possible matching.

Adoptive Families of America, Inc.
3333 Highway 100 North
Minneapolis, MN 55422
(612) 535-4829
Offers problem-solving assistance and information for adoptive and prospective adoptive families. 275 groups nationwide.

A.I.S. (Adoptees in Search)
P.O. Box 41016
Bethesda, MD 20824
(301) 656-8555
Provides help in finding birth parents for adoptees as well as assistance for adoptive and birth parents. Legislative activities work to end closed adoption records.

C.U.B. (Concerned United Birthparents)
2000 Walker St.
Des Moines, IA 50317
(800) 822-2777
Offers support for adoption-affected people in coping with adoption. Search assistance given in locating family members.

North American Council on Adoptable Children
970 Raymond Ave., #106
St. Paul, MN 55114-1146
(612) 644-3036
Maintains current listing of adoptive parent support groups and helps in starting new groups.

Operation Identity
13101 Blackstone Rd. NE
Albuquerque, NM 87111
(505) 293-3144
Mutual support and self-help organization embraces all facets of the adoption triad.

On-Line Information and Services

Adoption Advocates:
http://www.fpsol.com/adoption/advocates.html

Children, Youth, and Family Consortium Electronic Clearinghouse
http://www.cycf.umn.edu/adoptinfo.htp

Deaf Adoption News Service
newsgroup: sberke@netcom.com
Sends out information about deaf, hard of hearing, and possibly hearing impaired foreign children. To subscribe to the Deaf Adoption News Service send an e-mail message to sberke@netcom.com

Fact Sheet: Adoption Assistance and Foster Care
http://www.acf.dhhs.gov/ACFPrograms/FosterCare/foster.htm

Facts for Families
http://www.aacap.org/web/aacap/factsFam/
Educates parents and families about psychiatric disorders affecting children and adolescents (including adoption).

Help the Children
HTC1@aol.com
Adoption forum on Delphi called Future Adoptive Families and has also started a usenet group called alt.adoption.agency. Both groups are for preadoptive parents to speak with agencies and other adoption providers about the how-tos of adoption both domes-

tically and internationally, waiting children, and a few of the differences of parenting biological and adoptive children.

AGGRESSION AND ANGER

Children under age 18 are 244 percent more likely to be killed by gunshot wounds than people over 18.

General Information/Advocacy Groups

Building Conflict-Solving Skills
  Kansas Child Abuse Prevention Council
  715 SW 10th St.
  Topeka, KS 66612
  (913) 354-7738
  Goals are to decrease child abuse and neglect by educating elementary and middle school students, their parents, and teachers about conflict-solving skills.

Children's Safety Network National Resource Center
  National Injury and Violence Prevention Resource Centers
  (NCEMCH)
  Georgetown University
  2000 15th St. North, Suite 701
  Arlington, VA 22201-2617
  (703) 524-7802
  or
Education Development Center, Inc.
  55 Chapel St.
  Newton, MA 02158-1060
  (617) 969-7100

Community Youth Gang Service Project, Inc.
  144 S. Fetterly Ave.
  Los Angeles, CA 90022
  (213) 266-4264

Conflict Resolution Resources for Schools and Youth
  The Community Board Program
  1540 Market St., Room 490
  San Francisco, CA 94102
  (415) 552-1250

Council for Children with Behavioral Disorders
  1920 Association Dr.
  Reston, VA 22091
  (703) 620-3660
  Works to improve educational programs for children with emotional and behavioral disturbances.

ESR National Conflict Resolution Program
  Educators for Social Responsibility
  23 Garden St.
  Cambridge, MA 02138
  (617) 492-1764

Gang Intervention Program Youth Development, Inc.
  1710 Centro Familiar SW
  Albuquerque, NM 87105
  (505) 873-1604

Outreach and Tracking Program
  Old Colony YMCA
  15A Bolton Place
  Brockton, MA 02401
  (508) 584-1100

PACT Violence Prevention Project
  Contra Costa County Health Services Dept.
  75 Santa Barbara Rd.
  Pleasant Hill, CA 94523
  (510) 313-6000

Wholistic Stress Control Institute, Inc.
  P.O. Box 42481
  Atlanta, GA 30311
  (404) 344-2021 or (404) 755-0068
  (404) 755-4333 (Fax)
  Provides consultations, training, and educational resources on stress control, anger management, violence prevention, substance abuse prevention, and mental illness prevention. Develops training programs for educators, parents, children, and communities that increase coping skills and reduce the risk of high-risk behavior. Publications/training materials are available.

Hotlines/Helplines

Helping Parents
  (800) 747-6428

Self-Help/Support Groups

Children's Safety Network National
  National Injury and Violence Prevention Resource Centers (Parent Organization - NCEMCH)
  Georgetown University
  2000 15th St. N, Suite 701
  Arlington, VA 22201-2617
  (703) 524-7802

Peaceful Intervention Program
  (800) 779-7969
  Program designed to help anyone who deals with angry children. Offers an alternative to using physical restraint as a means of dealing with angry children.

Toughlove
  P.O. Box 1969
  Doylestown, PA 18901
  (215) 348-7090
  Self-help program for troubled families and angry children that depends on parents, professionals and other community members cooperatively rejecting destructive behavior and supporting new patterns of behavior. It runs a support network for more than 1,000 groups throughout the U.S. and Canada.

On-Line Information and Services

http://www.connix.com/~clearing/fangry.htm
Plain talk about dealing with the angry child.

http://www.ctw.org/0896/089612t1.htm
Developmental guide for children and anger.

AIDS/HIV

Every day in the U.S., 90 new cases of AIDS are identified and 60 people die from this fatal disease. AIDS has become the seventh leading cause of death for teens and young adults between the ages of 15 and 24 years.

—"Adolescent HIV/AIDS" by M. Greer, B. Armstrong & D. Dean in *Helping Children Grow Up in the '90s,* National Association of School Psychologists, 1992.

General Information/Advocacy Groups

CDC AIDS Clearinghouse
P.O. Box 6003
Rockville, MD 20850
(800) 458-5231
Offers reference and referral assistance, distributes AIDS/HIV educational materials, and maintains a database on AIDS service organizations and materials.

Children with AIDS Project of America
4141 Bethany Home Rd.
Phoenix, AZ 85019
(602) 973-4319 or (800) 866-AIDS

Pediatrics AIDS Foundation
1311 Colorado Ave.
Santa Monica, CA 90404
(310) 395-9051

Hotlines/Helplines

AIDS Clinical Trials Information Service
(800) TRIALS-A
(301) 217-0023 (International)
(800) 243-7012 (TDD/TTY)
(301) 738-6616 (Fax)

Immune Deficiency Foundation
(800) 296-4433
(410) 321-6647
(410) 321-9165 (Fax)
IDF@clark.net (e-mail)

Linea Nacional de SIDA
(800) 344-SIDA

National AIDS Hotline
(800) 342-AIDS
(800) 344-7432 - Spanish Service
(800) 243-7889 - (TDD)
Answers basic questions about HIV/AIDS (prevention, transmission, testing, health care, etc.)

National Minority AIDS Council
(800) 669-5052

Native American AIDS Information Line
(800) 283-2437
(510) 444-2051
(510) 444-1593 (Fax)

Project Inform
(800) 822-7422
(415) 558-8669
(415) 558-0684 (Fax)

Ryan White National Teen Education Program
(800) 933-KIDS

STD National Hotline
(800) 227-8922
Information on all sexually transmitted diseases, including AIDS.

TEENS T.A.P. (Teens Teaching AIDS Prevention)
(800) 234-TEEN
(816) 561-8784
(816) 561-9518 (TDD/TTY)
(816) 531-7199 (Fax)
Teen-staffed AIDS hotline Monday through Friday 4 to 8 p.m. CST; provides companions for children and adolescents with AIDS.

Self-Help/Support Groups

Bryan's House: A Project of Open Arms, Inc.
P.O. Box 191402
Dallas, TX 75219
(214) 559-3946
Responds to the needs of children and their families who are impacted by HIV/AIDS; provides medically-managed child care and community-based family support services.

Herbert G. Birch Services
  145-02 Farmers Blvd.
  Springfield Gardens, NY 11434
  (718) 528-5754
  Nonprofit agency provides life-enhancing support for developmentally disabled people and families of children with AIDS. Through special residential, educational, respite, and family programs, Birch Services enables children and adults to live their lives with dignity, joy, and respect.

National Association of People with AIDS
  1413 K St. NW
  Washington, DC 20005-3405
  (202) 898-0414
  Network of persons with AIDS to share information.

National Minority AIDS Council
  300 I St. NE
  Washington, DC 20002
  (202) 483-6622
  Organizes and develops AIDS groups in minority communities and publishes materials on AIDS. and its effect on minorities.

On-Line Information and Services

Candii Program
  http://www.itribe.net/candii/
  Nonprofit organization provides resources to children affected by HIV/AIDS: comprehensive medical, educational, social, financial and mental health services for children living with HIV/AIDS and support to their families.

Children with AIDS Project of America
  http://www.aids.kids.org/resource.html
  Provides resources pertaining to adoption and foster and respite care and for children with AIDS.

  http://www.familyvillage.wisc.edu/lib_aids.htm
  Resources, contacts, related web-sites, general information and the latest research on AIDS.

  pinform@hooked.net - (newsgroup)
  Internet Newsgroup on AIDS

ALCOHOL ABUSE

A recent national survey reported that 92 percent of high school seniors had tried alcohol. Each year, more than 7,000 teens die in alcohol-related car accidents, and another 40,000 are injured.

General Information/Advocacy Groups

American Council on Alcoholism, Inc.
  5024 Monroe St., Suite 110
  Rockville, MD 20850
  (800) 527-5344

National Addiction Referral Service
  5900 N. Granite Reef Rd., Suite 105
  Scottsdale, AZ 85250
  (800) 999-8731

National Center for Alcohol Education
  1601 N. Kent St.
  Arlington, VA 22209

National Clearinghouse for Alcohol and Drug Information
  P.O. Box 2345
  Rockville, MD 20847-2345
  (800) 729-6686
  NCADI is the main source for federal substance abuse information on prevention, education, research, treatment, and rehabilitation. Clearinghouse disseminates free publications, posters, video and audiotapes. Literature searches also are available as well as an on-line service and a publication catalog.

National Institute on Alcohol Abuse
  Parklawn Bldg.
  5600 Fishers La.
  Rockville, MD 20852
  (301) 443-3885

Hotlines/Helplines

Alcohol and Drug Abuse Helpline
   (800) 821-4357 or (800) 821-HELP
   Referrals to local alcohol and drug dependency units,
   and self-help groups.

American Council on Alcoholism
   (800) 527-5344
   (410) 889-0100
   (410) 889-0297 (Fax)

Families Anonymous
   (800) 736-9805
   (310) 313-5800
   (310) 313-6841 (Fax)

Mothers Against Drunk Driving
   (800) GET-MADD
   (214) 744-6233
   (214) 869-2206 (Fax)

Self-Help/Support Groups

Alateen
   Al-Anon Family Group Headquarters, Inc.
   P.O. Box 862, Midtown Station
   New York, NY 10018-0862
   (800) 356-9996
   (212) 302-7240
   (212) 869-3757 (Fax)
   National organization with numerous local chapters
   offers support and information to youth who have
   been affected by someone else's drinking.

Al-Anon and Alateen Family Group Headquarters
   World Service Office
   1600 Corporate Landing Pkwy.
   Virginia Beach, VA 23454-5617
   (800) 356-9996
   Family support groups are community resources for
   anyone whose life has been affected by an alcoholic
   problem drinker.

Alcoholics Anonymous World Services, Inc.
   General Service Office
   475 Riverside Dr., 11th Floor
   New York, NY 10115
   (212) 870-3400

National Asian Pacific American Families Against
Substance Abuse, Inc.
   1887 Maplegate St.
   Monterey Park, CA 91755
   (213) 278-0031
   (213) 278-9078 (Fax)

National Association for Native American Children of
Alcoholics
   1402 Third Ave., #1110
   Seattle, WA 98101-2118
   (206) 467-7686

National Association for the Dually Diagnosed
   110 Prince St.
   Kingston, NY 12401
   (800) 331-5362
   (914) 331-4569 (Fax)

On-Line Information and Services

CSAP: Alcohol, Tobacco, and Other Drugs Resource
Guide
   http://www.health.org/pubs/resguide/child.htm
   Publications and literature resources. Links to prevention material, studies, articles and reports and groups
   or organizations and programs.

Healthtouch On-line
   http://www.healthtouch.com/103821/103821.htm
   Directory listing of health organizations and government agencies that provide information on drug and
   alcohol abuse.

ANXIETY DISORDERS/ FEARS AND PHOBIAS

ANXIETY is a state of intense apprehension, uncertainty, and fear resulting from the anticipation of a threatening event or situation, often to a degree that the normal physical and psychological functioning of the affected individual is disrupted.

PHOBIA is characterized as a persistent, abnormal, or irrational fear of a specific thing or situation that compels one to avoid the feared stimulus. Avoidance or endurance of the phobic stimulus often results in intense anxiety and interference of normal routines or marked distress.

ANXIETY DISORDERS include the following:

Acute Stress Disorder
Agoraphobia
Generalized Anxiety Disorder
Obsessive-Compulsive Disorder
  (see also separate section)
Panic Attack
Post Traumatic Stress Disorder
  (see also separate section)
Social Phobia
Specific Phobia
Substance-Induced Anxiety Disorder

General Information/Advocacy Groups

Anxiety Disorders Association of America
  6000 Executive Blvd.
  Rockville, MD 20852
  (301) 231-9350
  (301) 231-7392 (Fax)
  Provides an information and referral service to help identify treatment facilities, local self-help groups, publications and membership information. A list of professionals in your state is available for $3. For information on professional treatment, local self-help groups, publications, and membership call (900) 737-3400 ($2 per minute).

National Anxiety Foundation
  3135 Custer Dr.
  Lexington, KY 40517
  (606) 272-7166

National Center for Post Traumatic Stress Disorder
  VA Medical and Regional Office Center
  215 N. Main St.
  White River Junction, VT 05009-0001
  (802) 296-5132

Panic Disorder Information Line
  National Institute of Mental Health
  Parklawn Bldg., Room 7-99
  5600 Fishers Lane
  Rockville, MD 20857
  (800) 647-2642
  A service of the NIMH, Information Line provides information about the panic disorder education program and distributes free publications on panic disorder for professionals and the general public.

Sidran Foundation
  2328 W. Joppa Rd., Suite 15
  Lutherville, MD 21093
  (410) 825-8888
  sidran@access.digex.net (e-mail)
  Provides information and advocates in support of people who have experienced trauma and have trauma-related disorders. Develops public education workshops on the psychological outcomes of severe childhood trauma for adult survivors, partners, caregivers, and professionals. Publishes books and educational materials on traumatic stress disorders, dissociative disorders, child sexual abuse, ritual abuse, self-injury, and self-help/recovery.

Hotlines/Helplines

National Institute of Mental Health Panic Disorders Hotline
  (800) 64-PANIC

Self-Help/Support Groups

ABIL, Inc.
    1418 Lorraine Ave.
    Richmond, VA 23227
    (804) 353-3964
    Offers mutual support for persons with agoraphobia, anxiety, or panic-related disorders and their families.

Agoraphobics in Motion (A.I.M.)
    1729 Crooks St.
    Royal Oak, MI 48067
    (810) 547-0400

Depressives Anonymous
    329 E. 62nd St.
    New York, NY 10021
    (212) 689-2600
    Helps anxious and depressed persons change troublesome behavior patterns and attitudes about living.

Freedom From Fear
    308 Seaview Ave.
    Staten Island, NY 10305
    (718) 351-1717

PASS-Group, Inc.
    6 Mahogany Dr.
    Williamsville, NY 14221
    (716) 689-4399
    Formerly the Panic Attack Sufferers' Support Group, PASS-Group helps people with anxiety disorders such as panic attacks, agoraphobia, and related phobias. It provides telephone counseling, referrals to nationwide groups, and information.

Phobics Anonymous
    P.O. Box 1180
    Palm Springs, CA 92263
    (619) 322-COPE
    Provides fellowship for people with anxiety and panic disorders following the 12-step program of recovery.

On-Line Information and Services

Anxiety, Panic and Stress
    http://www.onlinepsych.com/treat/Anxiety_Panic_and_
    Stress.htm
    Links to resources of all kinds relating to anxiety, panic and stress.

The Anxious Child
    http://www.psych.med.umich.edu/web/aacap/factsfam/anxious.htm
    Fact sheet for families dealing with anxious children.

Facts 4 Families - The Anxious Child
    http://www.cmhc.com/factsfam/anxious.htm
    Fact sheet from The American Academy of Child and Adolescent Psychiatry

Mental Health Net Guide to Anxiety Disorders
    http://www.cmhc.com/guide/anxiety.htm
    Self-help resources on diagnosing and treating anxiety disorders. Includes fact sheets and resources for professional help.

ATTENTION DEFICIT DISORDER (with or without Hyperactivity)

ATTENTION-DEFICIT/HYPERACTIVITY DISORDER (ADHD) is characterized by a persistent pattern of inattention and/or hyperactivity-impulsivity that is more frequent and severe than is observed in children at a comparable level of development. A collection of problems impair the child's ability to regulate his or her behavior, including inattention and distractibility, impulsivity or difficulty in controlling behavior, difficulty with rule-governed behavior leading to the need for increased levels of feedback from the environment, hyperactivity or overarousal, and difficulty in maintaining a consistent level of performance.

General Information/Advocacy Groups

Attention Deficit Disorder Association
 P.O. Box 488
 West Newbury, MA 01985
 (800) 487-2282
 Provides resource information, support, and advocacy for people with ADD; distributes publications, sponsors conferences, and provides referrals to support groups; offers a Fax-On-Demand system for fast dissemination of materials.

A.D.D. WareHouse
 300 NW 70th Ave.
 Plantation, FL 33317
 (800) 233-9273
 Makes available Attention Deficit Disorder materials for educators to help students; programs to help parents and teachers build self-esteem; information on medication, behavior modification, and cognitive strategies for health care professionals; and books and videos for children and young teens.

Attention Deficit Information Network
 475 Hillside Ave.
 Needham, MA 02194
 (617) 455-9895
 Offers support groups and information to families of children with ADD, adults with ADD, and profession-

als through a network of chapters across the country; has information on training programs and speakers for those who work with individuals with ADD; list of publications also available.

Hotlines/Helplines

Attention Deficit Disorder Hotline
 (800) 254-8081

Challenge
 (800) ADD-2322
 (508) 462-0495
 (508) 462-0495 (Fax, press 5* after the tone)

National Attention Deficit Disorder Association
 (800) 487-2282

Self-Help/Support Groups

Children and Adults with Attention Deficit Disorder (CH.A.D.D.)
 499 NW 70th Ave.
 Plantation, FL 33317
 (305) 587-3700
 CH.A.D.D. serves people affected by ADD on local, state, and national levels; offers information, such as research and treatment of ADD, through newsletters and other publications. Local chapters sponsor parent support groups, convene meetings featuring speakers, and work with local school systems to ensure appropriate educational services for children.

On-Line Information and Services

Attention Deficit WWW Archive
 http://www.seas.upenn.edu/~mengwong/add/
 Information resource on many aspects of ADD and ADHD.

Internet Newsgroup Discussing ADD/ADHD.
 alt.support.attn-deficit

AUTISM

AUTISM is characterized by the presence of markedly abnormal or impaired development in social interaction and communication and a particularly limited repertoire of activity and interests. Manifestations of the disorder vary greatly, depending on the developmental level and age of the child. Autism is sometimes referred to as early infantile autism, childhood autism, or Kanner's autism.

General Information/Advocacy Groups

Autism Society of America
7910 Woodmont Ave., Suite 650
Bethesda, MD 20814
(301) 657-0881 or (800) 328-8476
(301)657-0869 (Fax)
Web site: http://www.autism-society.org/
Largest support organization for autistic children offers such services as membership in over 200 local or state chapters, annual national meeting, mail-order bookstore, and information and referral system to answer questions about topics ranging from insurance to model treatment programs to identifying local support groups, a quarterly newsletter *The Advocate,* and policy and lobbying activities to legislate better services for autistic children and adults.

Autism Support Center
64 Holten St.
Danvers, MA 01923
(508) 777-9135
Resource library and guidance center.

Institute for Child Behavior Research
4182 Adams Ave.
San Diego, CA 92116
(619) 281-7165
Provides information and research findings on autism and related learning and behavior disorders.

Hotlines/Helplines

Autism Society of America
(800) 3-AUTISM

Self-Help/Support Groups

(see Autism Society of America)

On-Line Information and Services

Autism Resources
http://web.syr.edu:80/~jmwobus/autism
Index of on-line info on Autism and Asperger's Syndrome.

Autism Society of America
http://www.autism-society.org/
Resources for helping individuals with autism and their families through advocacy, education, public awareness and research.

Zia Austic Disorder - Autism Resources The Best of Health Information on The Net
http://www.zia.com/health1/mental-health/symptoms-and-diseases/autistic-disorderautism/
Resources including organizations and newsgroups about autism and related topics.

CHILD ABUSE AND NEGLECT

In the U.S. each day, approximately 8,500 children are reported abused or neglected.

General Information/Advocacy Groups

American Association for Protecting Children
   American Humane Association
   63 Inverness Dr. East
   Englewood, CO 80112-5117
   (303) 792-9900

Center for Child Protection
   Children's Hospital
   3020 Children's Way
   San Diego, CA 92123
   (619) 974-8017

Childhelp USA
   1345 North Elcentro Ave.
   Hollywood, CA 90028
   (213) 465-4016
   Provides 24-hour hotline staffed by crisis intervention counselors, residential treatment for children aged 2-12, foster home placement services, therapy for adult survivors of child abuse and dysfunctional families, and training for child care workers and foster parents. Conducts research on child abuse and distributes educational materials.

Child Welfare League of America
   440 First St. NW, Suite 310
   Washington, DC 20001-2085
   (202) 638-2952
   (202) 638-4004 (Fax)
   National consortium of numerous organizations offers information, support, and referrals related to abused and neglected children and their families, family preservation, child care, foster care, adoption, residential group homes, teens who are parents or pregnant. Child Welfare League offers a wide array of publications on these issues.

Children's Rights Council
   220 I St. NE, Suite 230
   Washington, DC 20002
   (202) 547-6227

Committee for Children
   172 20th Ave.
   Seattle, WA 98122
   (206) 343-1223

Family Violence and Sexual Assault Institute
   1310 Clinic Dr.
   Tyler, TX 75701
   (903) 595-6600

International Society for Prevention of Child Abuse and Neglect
   1205 Oneida St.
   Denver, CO 80220
   (303) 321-3963

National CASA
   The National CASA Association
   100 W. Harrison, Suite 500
   North Tower
   Seattle, WA 98119
   (800) 628-3233
   Nonprofit organization of court-appointed volunteers who advocate for children in court.

National Clearinghouse on Child Abuse and Neglect Information
   P.O. Box 1182
   Washington, DC 20013-1182
   (800) 394-3366
   (703) 385-3206 (Fax)
   Resource for child maltreatment. Information on prevention, identification, investigation, and treatment of child abuse is developed and disseminated. Products and services available include publications, database searches, annotated bibliographies, fact sheets, resource listings, references and referrals.

National Committee to Prevent Child Abuse
   332 S. Michigan Ave., Suite 1600
   Chicago, IL 60604-4357
   (312) 663-3520

National Council on Child Abuse and Family Violence
1155 Connecticut Ave. NW, Suite 400
Washington, DC 20036
(202) 429-6695

Sidran Foundation
2328 W. Joppa Rd., Suite 15
Lutherville, MD 21093
(410) 825-8888
sidran@access.digex.net (e-mail)
Provides information and advocates in support of people who have experienced trauma and have trauma-related disorders. Develops public education workshops on the psychological outcomes of severe childhood trauma for adult survivors, partners, caregivers, and professionals. Publishes books and educational materials on traumatic stress disorders, dissociative disorders, child sexual abuse, ritual abuse, self-injury, and self-help/recovery.

Hotlines/Helplines

American Humane Association Children's Hotline
(800) 227-4645

Childhelp/IOF Foresters National Child Abuse Hotline
(800) 4-A-CHILD
(800) 2-A-CHILD (TDD)

National Child Abuse Hotline
(800) 422-4453
Crisis hotline for children and adolescents experiencing abuse.

National Committee to Prevent Child Abuse
Information Line
(800) 55-NCPCA
(312) 663-3520
(312) 665-3540 (TDD/TTY)

National Council on Child Abuse and Family Violence
(800) 222-2000

Parents Anonymous
(800) 421-0353
Helpline for parents who fear they may abuse their children.

Youth Crisis Hotline
(800) 448-4663
Hotline for children/adolescents who are runaways, experiencing abuse, or contemplating suicide.

Self-Help/Support Groups

Childhelp USA
1345 Elcentro Ave.
Hollywood, CA 90028
(213) 465-4016
Maintains a national network of volunteer chapters.

Giarretto Institute
Daughters and Sons United/Parents United
232 E. Gish Rd.
San Jose, CA 95112
(408) 453-7616

Parents Anonymous
675 W. Foothill Blvd., Suite 220
Claremont, CA 91711
(909) 621-6184
National program to help parents learn how to avoid abusive or harmful behavior; runs a network of over 2,000 groups throughout the U.S.

On-Line Information and Services

Child Abuse Prevention Network
http://child.cornell.edu/
Network of information dedicated to enhancing resources for the prevention of child abuse and neglect.

Cycle of Violence Revisited
http://www.ncjrs.org/txtfiles/cyclepre.txt
NCJ research article that explores what happens to abused and neglected children after they grow up.

Needy People Foundation
http://www.register.com/needy
Links to services and programs sponsored by the Needy People Foundation for neglected and abused adults and children.

CHRONIC ILLNESS

Cancer strikes 14 out of 10,000 children in the U.S. every year, primarily in the preschool years. Leukemia is the most common childhood malignancy, with an incidence of 4 in 10,000.

> —"Children and Cancer" by V. Van de Water in *Childrens' Needs: Psychological Perspectives*, National Association of School Psychologists, 1987.

General Information/Advocacy Groups

Candlelighters Childhood Cancer Foundation
7910 Woodmont Ave., Suite 460
Bethesda, MD 20814-3015
(800) 366-2223
(301) 657-8401
(301) 718-2686 (Fax)
75717.3513@compuserve.com (e-mail)
International, nonprofit organization provides information and referrals, education, support, database searches, publications, and advocacy for families of children of cancer, survivors of childhood cancer, and practitioners. Network of parent support groups in all U.S. states and on every continent links parents with meetings, speakers, conferences, other parents, summer camps, transportation, emergency funding, and publications. No membership charge.

Center for Children with Chronic Illness and Disabilities
Box 721-UMHC
420 Delaware St.
Minneapolis, MN 55455
(612) 626-4032
Voice/TDD: (612) 624-3939
(612) 626-2134 (Fax)

National Chronic Pain Outreach Association
4922 Hampden La.
Bethesda, MD 20814
(301) 652-4948

National Head Injury Foundation Family Helpline
(800) 444-6443
(202) 296-8850 (Fax)
Provides information and resources for people with head injury, their families, and the professionals who provide rehabilitative care; offers educational material on the impact of brain injury, location of rehabilitative facilities, and availability of community services and also promotes activities related to the prevention of head injuries.

National Headache Foundation
428 W. St James Pl., 2nd Floor
Chicago, IL 60614
(800) 843-2256

National Parent to Parent Support and Information System
P.O. Box 907
Blue Ridge, GA 30513
(800) 651-1151
Links parents of children with rare disorders or special health care needs.

Hotlines/Helplines

Alliance of Genetic Support Groups
(800) 336-GENE
(301) 652-5553
(301) 654-0171 (Fax)

ALM International
Information about Hansen's disease.
(800) 543-3131

ALS Association (Amyotrophic Lateral Sclerosis)
Information on Lou Gehrig's Disease
(800) 782-4747
(818) 340-7500
(818) 340-7573 (TDD)
(818) 340-2060 (Fax)

American Association of Kidney Patients
(800) 749-2257
(813) 223-7099
(813) 223-0001 (Fax)

American Brain Tumor Association
(800) 886-2282
(708) 827-9910
(708) 827-9918 (Fax)

American Cancer Society
  (800) ACS-2345
  (404) 325-2217 (Fax)

American Council of the Blind
  (800) 424-8666
  (202) 467-5081

American Foundation for the Blind
  (800) 232-5463
  (212) 620-2147

American Heart Association
  (800) AHAUSAI
  (214) 706-1341 (Fax)
  http:www.amhrt.org (Internet)

American Kidney Fund
  (800) 638-8299
  (301) 881-3052 (or -3053 or -3054)
  (301) 881-0898 (Fax)

American Liver Foundation
  (800) 223-0179
  (201) 256-2550
  (201) 256-3214 (Fax)

American Lung Association
  (800) LUNG-USA
  (313) 973-6730
  (313) 973-6115 (Fax)

American Lupus Society
  (800) 331-1802
  (805) 339-0443
  (805) 339-0467 (Fax)

Better Hearing Institute
  (800) EAR-WELL (U.S. and Canada)
  (800) EAR-WELL (TDD/TTY)
  (703) 750-9302 (Fax)

Bill Burton Free Hospital Care
  Information for free or minimal cost hospital care.
  (800) 638-0742
  (301) 443-8225
  (800) 492-0359 (MD)
  (301) 443-0619 (Fax)

Blind Children's Center
  (800) 222-3566
  (800) 222-3567 (CA)
  (213) 665-3828 (Fax)

Cancer Connection
  (800) 678-8868 (Fax)
  amercurio@smtplink.coh.org (e-mail)

Cancer Information Service
  (800) 4-CANCER

Children's Craniofacial Association
  (800) 535-3643
  (214) 994-9902
  (214) 994-9831 (Fax)

Cleft Palate Foundation
  (800) 242-5338
  (412) 481-0847 (Fax)

Cornelia de Lange Syndrome Foundation
  (800) 223-8355
  (800) 753-2357
  (203) 692-0159
  (203) 693-6819 (Fax)

Cystic Fibrosis Foundation
  (800) FIGHT-CF

Deafness Research Foundation
  (800) 535-3323

Dial-a-Hearing Screening Test
  (800) 222-EARS

Ear Foundation
  (800) 545-HEAR
  (615) 329-7849 (TDD)
  (615) 329-7935 (Fax)

Epilepsy Foundation of America
  (800) 332-1000
  (301) 459-3700
  (800) 332-2070 (TDD/TTY)
  (301) 577-4941 (Fax)

Guardians of Hydrocephalus Research
(800) 458-8655
(718) 743-GHRF
(718) 743-1171 (Fax)

Guide Dog Foundation for the Blind, Inc.
(800) 548-4337
(516) 361-5192 (Fax)
GuideDogFoundation@GuideDog.org (e-mail)

Hear Now
(800) 648-HEAR
(303) 695-7797
(800) 648-HEAR (TDD)
(303) 695-7797 (TDD)
(303) 695-7789 (Fax)

Hearing Aid Helpline
(800) 622-EARS

Immune Deficiency Foundation
(800) 296-4433
(410) 321-6647
(410) 321-9165 (Fax)
IDF@clark.net (e-mail)

Juvenile Diabetes Foundation International: Diabetes Research Foundation
(800) 533-2873
(800) 223-1138
(212) 889-7575 (NY)

Kidneywatch
(800) 994-9973

Leukemia Society of America Public Information Resource Line
(800) 955-4LSA

Make Today Count
(800) 432-2273
Links people with life-threatening illnesses for mutual support.

National Association for Parents of the Visually Impaired
(800) 562-6265
(617) 972-7441
(617) 972-7444

National Association of Hospital Hospitality Houses
Information and referral service identifies lodging facilities near the hospital where one has been referred for treatment.
(800) 542-9730
(317) 288-3226
(317) 287-0321 (Fax)

National Down Syndrome Congress
(800) 232-NDSC
(404) 633-2817 (Fax)

National Down Syndrome Society
(800) 221-4602

National Foundation for Facial Reconstruction
(800) 422-3223
(202) 263-6656
(212) 263-7534 (Fax)

National Fragile X Foundation
(800) 688-8765
(303) 333-6155
(303) 333-4369 (Fax)

National Headache Foundation
(800) 445-4808 or (800) 843-2256

National Information Clearinghouse for Infants with Disabilities and Life-Threatening Conditions
(800) 922-9234, ext. 201
(800) 922-9234 (TDD/TTY)
(803) 777-5058 (Fax)

National Kidney Foundation
(800) 622-9010

National Mafran Foundation
(800) 8-MAFRAN
(516) 883-0721
(516) 883-8712 (Fax)

National Marrow Donor Program
(800) MARROW-2
(612) 627-5899 (Fax)

National Organization for Rare Disorders
  (800) 999-6673
  (203) 746-6518 (CT)
  (203) 746-6927 (TDD/TTY)
  (203) 746-6481 (Fax)

National Tour Association
  Handicapped Travel Division
  (800) NTA-8886

Phoenix Society for Burn Survivors
  (800) 888-BURN
  (215) 946-4788 (Fax)

Shriner's Hospital Referral Line
  Information and referral service for free hospital care
  at a local Shriner hospital for children who suffer from
  orthopedic problems or burns.
  (800) 237-5055
  (813) 281-0300, ext. 3088
  (800) 361-7256 (Canada)
  (813) 281-8496 (Fax)

St. Jude's Children's Research Hospital
  (800) 877-5833
  (901) 522-9733
  (901) 523-6600 (Fax)

Tripod Grapevine
  Information and referral service for issues related to
  deafness.
  (800) 352-8888
  (800) 2-TRIPOD (CA)
  (800) 352-8888 (TDD)
  (800) 2-TRIPOD (TDD) (CA)

United Cerebral Palsy Association, Inc.
  (800) 872-5827
  (202) 776-0406
  (202) 973-7197 (TDD)
  (202) 776-0414 (Fax)
  UCPAPS@aol.com (e-mail)

United Leukodystrophy Foundation
  (800) 728-5483
  (815) 895-3211
  (815) 895-2432 (Fax)
  ULF@ceet.niu.edu (e-mail)

Self-Help/Support Groups

MATRIX, A Parent Network and Resource Center
  320 Nova Albion Way
  San Rafael, CA 94903
  (415) 499-3877
  Acts as a support, information and resource center for
  parents who have discovered their child has a disability or special need. Support is offered by parents who
  have gone through a similar process.

TASK (Team of Advocates for Special Kids)
  100 West Cerritos
  Anaheim, CA 92805
  (714) 533-TASK
  Provides services, information, support, training, legal
  information, advocacy, workshops, and referrals for
  families of children with disabilities; provides specialized services to disabled children of Vietnam Veterans.

Touchstone Support Network
  378 Cambridge Ave., Suite K
  Palo Alto, CA 94306
  (414) 328-4495
  E-mail: http://www-med.stanford.edu/touchstone/.
  Provides support for children with terminal illness.

On-Line Information and Services

EDMARC - Hospice for Children
  http://www.whro.org/cl/Edmarc/index.htm/
  Information and services provided by Edmarc Hospice
  for children, whose mission is to serve families with
  children who have a life-threatening illness.

Kids-only Newsgroups: CaringKids is for kids who
know someone who is dealing with an illness; SickKids
is for kids who are themselves sick. To subscribe send
e-mail to:
  listserv@sjuvm.stjohns.edu
  subject: blank
  Message: subscribe CaringKids FirstName LastName
           subscribe SickKids FirstName LastName

Newsgroups for parents: The Caring Parent List is for adults who want to discuss kids with serious illnesses. To subscribe send e-mail to:

    listserv@sjuvm.stjohns.edu
    subject: blank
    Message: subscribe CaringParents FirstName LastName

COMMUNICATION DISORDERS

STUTTERING is a disturbance in the normal fluency and time patterning of speech that is inappropriate for the individual's age. It is characterized by speaking with a spasmodic repetition or prolongation of sounds. This disturbance interferes with academic achievement and social communication.

SELECTIVE MUTISM is the persistent failure to speak in social situations (i.e., at school or with playmates) where speaking is expected, despite speaking in other situations. This disturbance interferes with academic achievement and social communication. Gestures, nodding or shaking the head, or pulling or pushing may be the means of communication.

General Information/Advocacy Groups

National Center for Stuttering
    200 E. 33rd St., #17C
    New York, NY 10016
    (800) 221-2483
    Promotes information and treatment for stutterers and parents of very young children who are beginning to show signs of stuttering.

Sertoma International/Sertoma Foundation
    1912 East Meyer Blvd.
    Kansas City, MO 64132
    (816) 333-8300
    Provides information and resources to people with speech and hearing disabilities.

Hotlines/Helplines

American Speech
    (800) 638-8255

Stuttering Foundation of America
    (800) 992-9392
    Information and referrals for stutters and professionals; phone support, conferences, referral list of speech pathologists who specialize in stuttering.

Stuttering Resource Foundation
(800) 232-4773

Self-Help/Support Groups

American Speech-Language-Hearing Association
10801 Rockville Pike
Rockville, MD 20852
(301) 897-5700

Center for Stuttering Therapy
1570 Oak Ave.
Evanston, IL 60201
(847) 864-8289

National Stuttering Project
2151 Irving St., #208
San Francisco, CA 94122-1609
(800) 364-1677
Self-help chapter meetings provide supportive environment in which people who stutter can learn to communicate more effectively. 65 groups nationwide.

Speak Easy International Foundation, Inc.
233 Concord Dr.
Paramus, NJ 07652
(201) 262-0895
Self-help groups for adult and adolescent stutterers.

Stuttering Resource Foundation
123 Oxford Rd.
New Rochelle, NY 10804
(914) 632-3925 or (800) 232-4773
Publishes books about stuttering, organizes support groups for parents of children who stutter or are at risk of stuttering, and provides an information and referral service to parents and practitioners throughout the U.S. and Canada.

On-Line Information and Services

Guide to Exceptional Children - Speech and Language Impairment
http://mrcohen1.keel.physics.ship.edu/~jak/speech.html
Links to speech and language disorder resources for children.

Ontario Association for Families of Children with Communication Disorders
http://www.ncf.carleton.ca/freenet/rootdir/menus/schools/comm-disorders/about
Provides information, education and support to families of children with communication disorders.

CONDUCT DISORDER

CONDUCT DISORDER is characterized by a child's persistent pattern of behavior in which the basic rights of others or major age-appropriate societal norms or rules are violated. Behaviors include aggressive conduct that causes or threatens physical harm to other people or animals, nonaggressive behavior that causes property damage or loss, deceitfulness or theft, and serious violations of rules. These behaviors usually cause impairment in social and academic functioning.

General Information/Advocacy Groups

Juvenile Justice Clearinghouse
    P.O. Box 6000
    Rockville, MD 20850
    (800) 638-8736

National Criminal Justice Reference Service
    P.O. Box 6000
    Rockville, MD 20850
    (800) 851-3420

National GAINS Center for People with Co-Occurring Disorders in the Justice System
    Policy Research Associates, Inc.
    262 Delaware Ave.
    Delmar, NY 12054
    (800) 311-4246
    Collects and disseminates information about effective mental health and substance abuse services for people with co-occurring disorders who come in contact with the criminal justice system. Provides technical assistance to communities for the establishment and implementation of services for individuals in the justice system. The center is sponsored by Substance Abuse and Mental Health Services Administration (SAMHSA) and the National Institute of Corrections.

Self-Help/Support Groups

Parents Involved Network
    311 S. Juniper St., Room 902
    Philadelphia, PA 19107
    (800) 688-4226 Ext. 250
    Parent-run, self-help/advocacy, information, and referral for families of children/adolescents who have emotional or behavioral disorders.

Toughlove
    P.O. Box 1969
    Doylestown, PA 18901
    (215) 348-7090
    Self-help program for troubled families and angry children that depends on parents, professionals and other community members cooperatively rejecting destructive behavior and supporting new patterns of behavior. It runs a support network for more than 1,000 groups throughout the U.S. and Canada.

On-Line Information and Services

Conduct Disorders in Children and Adolescent FACT SHEET
    http://www.mentalhealth.org/CHILD/CONDUCT.HTM
    Fact sheet produced by The Center for Mental Health Services

Conduct Disorders
    http://www.psych.med.umich.edu//web/aacap/factsFam/conduct.htm
    Fact Sheet created by The American Academy of Child and Adolescent Psychiatry.

Conduct Disorder
    http://www-adm.pdx.edu/user/rri/rtc/resource/conduct.htm
    Description, symptoms, diagnosis and references prepared by The Research and Training Center on Family Support and Childrens Mental Health

Mental Health Net: Conduct Disorders
    http://www.cmhcsys.com/factsfam/conduct.htm
    Treatment Programs for Conduct Disordered Children

DEATH/BEREAVEMENT

Five percent of children, or 1.5 million, in the U.S. lose one or both parents by the time they reach age 15. Bereaved children under age 5 are more susceptible than older children to pathological outcomes.

General Information/Advocacy Groups

Association of Death Education and Counseling
 638 Prospect Ave.
 Hartford, CT 06105
 (203) 586-7503
 Addresses dying, death, and bereavement issues from the professional's perspective. Membership benefits include the bimonthly newsletter *The Forum*; discounted subscriptions to journals including *Death Studies, Omega - Journal of Death and Dying, Bereavement Magazine, Thanatos, Illness, Crises and Loss*, and *The Thanatology Newsletter*; access to a wide array of printed materials on death and dying through the association's book service; and discounted registration fees to the ADEC Annual National Conference and Education Institute Programs.

Circle of Care
 2200 N. Classen, Suite 1420
 Oklahoma City, OK 73106
 (800) 528-1906

Good Grief Program
 Judge Baker Children's Center
 295 Longwood Ave.
 Boston, MA 02115
 (617) 232-8390
 Helps schools and community groups become a base of support for children when a friend dies.

Grieving Well Center
 P.O. Box 622256
 Orlando, FL 32862
 (407) 895-9285

Pet Loss/The Delta Society
 P.O. Box 1080
 Renton, WA 98057
 (206) 226-7357

Hotlines/Helplines

Grief Recovery Helpline
 (800) 445-4508
 Provides educational services on recovering from loss.

Self-Help/Support Groups

Compassionate Friends
 P.O. Box 3696
 Oak Brook, IL 60522-3696
 (708) 990-0010
 Sponsors support groups across the country for parents, siblings, and friends grieving the death of a child.

On-Line Information and Services

Newsgroup discussing Grief
 alt.support.grief

Bereaved Parents' Resources on the Internet
 http://www.rivendell.org/parents.net.html
 Links to resources for parents who have lost a child.

Edmarc Hospice and Bereavement Program
 http://www.whro.org/cl/Edmarc/hospice.html
 Project M.A.G.I.C. (My Active Grieving Instills Courage) is a customized and comprehensive program of support available to any family who has experienced the death of a child.

For other resources:
 http://members.aol.com/handinfo1/resource.html

Sharing and Caring News and Information
 http://www1.aksi.net/~cmark/sac.htm
 Support group for children who are grieving for a murdered family member.

DEPRESSION

DEPRESSION is defined as a psychotic or neurotic condition characterized by an inability to concentrate, by insomnia, and by feelings of extreme sadness, dejection, and hopelessness. Symptoms may include depressed or irritable mood, marked diminished pleasure in daily activities, significant weight loss or weight gain, insomnia or hypersomnia on a nearly daily basis, psychomotor retardation or agitation on an almost daily basis, fatigue or loss of energy on an almost daily basis, feelings of worthlessness and/or excessive guilt on an almost daily basis, decreased concentration, indecisiveness, and recurrent thoughts of death and/or suicidality.

General Information/Advocacy Groups

Depression After Delivery
  P.O. Box 1282
  Morrisville, PA 19067
  (215) 295-3994

Depression Awareness/Recognition/Treatment Program (D/ART)
  National Institute of Mental Health (NIMH)
  5600 Fishers Lane
  Rockville, MD 20857
  (301) 443-4513
  (800) 421-4211
  National campaign to increase awareness and education on depressive disorders for the general public, primary care providers, and mental health specialists. The program offers several free brochures and publications. The publications list is available from the program and the National Institute of Mental Health.

DRADA (Depressive Disorders)
  Johns Hopkins Hospital Meyer 3-181
  600 N. Wolfe St.
  Baltimore, MD 21287
  (410) 955-4647

Lithium Information Center
  Dean Foundation
  800 Excelsior Dr., Suite 302
  Madison, WI 53717-1914
  (608) 836-8070
  Provides biomedical and general information about lithium and other treatments for bipolar (manic-depressive) disorder; offers referrals to local medical professionals and support groups. Written materials are available for a fee.

National Alliance for Research on Schizophrenia and Depression
  60 Cutter Mill Rd., Suite 200
  Great Neck, NY 10029
  (516) 829-0091

National Depressive and Manic Depressive Association
  730 N. Franklin St., Suite 501
  Chicago, IL 60601
  (800) 826-3632

National Foundation for Depressive Illness
  P.O. Box 2257
  New York, NY 10116
  (800) 248-4344
  (212) 268-4434 (Fax)

Paxil Access to Care Program
  (800) 729-4544
  Provides eligible consumers with free or low-cost supplies of the antidepressant medication Paxil.

Hotlines/Helplines

Seasonal Affective Disorder Hotline
  (212) 960-5714

Self-Help/Support Groups

Depressed Anonymous
  1013 Wagner Ave.
  Louisville, KY 40217
  (502) 569-1989
  Offers 12-step program to help depressed people believe and hope they can feel better.

Depressives Anonymous
  329 East 62nd St.
  New York, NY 10021
  (212) 689-2600
  Helps anxious and depressed persons change trouble-some behavior patterns and attitudes about living.

On-Line Information and Services

alt.support.depression (Newsgroup)

Mental Health Net - Depression Sel-Help Resources
  http://www.cmhc.com/guide/depress.htm
  A guide of diagnostic treatment resources for depression.

http://earth.execpc.com/~corbeau/depress.html
Depression links newsgroups and mailing lists, articles, medication, choosing a psychologist, etc. pertaining to depression

DIVORCE

Almost half of all marriages will end in divorce, and 40 to 50 percent of all children born in the past decade will spend some time living in a single-parent family.
  —"Children and Divorce" by S. Royal and H. Knoff in *Helping Children Grow Up in the '90s,* National Association of School Psychologists, 1992.

General Information/Advocacy Groups

American Association of Marriage and Family Therapists
  110 17th St. NW, 10th Floor
  Washington, DC 20036
  (202) 452-0109

Center for Mediation and Law
  34 Forrest St.
  Mill Valley, CA 92941
  (415) 383-1300

Resource Center on Child Protection and Custody in Domestic Violence Situations
  P.O. Box 8970
  Reno, NV 89507
  (800) 527-3223
  Provides information, materials, consultation, technical assistance, and legal research related to child protection and custody within the context of domestic violence. Publications list is available.

Single Parent Resource Center
  141 W. 28th St., #302
  New York, NY 10001
  (212) 951-7030

Society of Professionals in Dispute Resolution
  815 15th St. NW, Suite 530
  Washington, DC 20005
  (202) 783-7277

Self-Help/Support Groups

Joint Custody Association
  10606 Wilkins Ave.
  Los Angeles, CA 90024
  (310) 475-5352
  Assists divorcing parents and their families to achieve joint custody.

National Fathers Network
  Kindering Center
  16120 NE 8th St.
  Bellevue, WA 98008-3937
  (206) 747-4004

On-Line Information and Services

alt.support.divorce
  Newsgroup discussing divorce.

Children at Risk Today
  http://www.curbet.com/cart

Self-Help Improvement On-line - Divorce Information
  http://www.selfgrowth.com/divorce.html:
  Complete list of divorce sites

DOMESTIC VIOLENCE

In homes where domestic violence occurs, children are abused at a rate of 1,500 percent higher than the national average.
  —National Coalition Against Domestic Violence

General Information/Advocacy Groups

Center for Prevention of Sexual and Domestic Violence
  1914 N. 34th St., Suite 200
  Seattle, WA 98103-9058
  (206) 634-1903
  Inter-religious organization serves as an educational resource working specifically with religious communities on issues of sexual abuse and domestic violence. It works to train and educate clergy and lay people to recognize domestic violence and to support the victims. Publications are available.

Family Violence and Sexual Assault Institute
  1310 Clinic Dr.
  Tyler, TX 75701
  (903) 595-6600

National Battered Women's Law Project
  799 Broadway, Room 402
  New York, NY 10003
  (212) 741-9480

National Coalition Against Domestic Violence
  P.O. Box 34103
  Washington, DC 20043-4103
  (202) 638-6388
  Advocacy and training organization dedicated to preventing domestic violence and improving the lives of battered women. It offers publications, posters, and videotapes as well as a directory of programs nationwide. A publications list is available. Offices also are located in Colorado.

National Council on Child Abuse and Family Violence
  1155 Connecticut Ave. NW, Suite 400
  Washington, DC 20036
  (202) 429-6695

National Resource Center for Domestic Violence
6400 Flank Dr., Suite 1300
Harrisburg, PA 17112
(800) 537-2238
Promotes research, policy analysis, and program development with the goal of strengthening the existing system for battered women. Provides statistics, fact sheets, information packets, training materials, and technical assistance. Three special interest centers focus on civil and criminal justice issues, child protection and custody issues, and health care access for battered women and their children.

National Victim Center
2111 Wilson Blvd., Suite 300
Arlington, VA 22201
(703) 276-2880
Provides information packets, fact sheets, and statistics on victimization; offers referrals to local support groups for people who have been victims.

Resource Center on Child Protection and Custody in Domestic Violence Situations
P.O. Box 8970
Reno, NV 89507
(800) 527-3223
Provides information, materials, consultation, technical assistance, and legal research related to child protection and custody within the context of domestic violence. A publications list is available.

Hotlines/Helplines

National Domestic Violence Hotline
(800) 799-7233

Self-Help/Support Groups

Batterers Incorporated
6243 Fallard Dr.
Upper Marlborough, MD 20772
(800) 638-0224
Program for men who wish to control their anger and eliminate abusive behavior toward women.

On-Line Information and Services

Mental Health Links - Domestic Abuse
http://www.bconnex.net/~dsneyd/resource.html
Wife abuse resource.

Save Yourself from Domestic Violence
http://www.saveyourself.com/dvc.html
Legal aid and advice.

Violence Links
http://www.abacon.com/sociology/soclinks/violence.html
Resources and information.

DRUG ABUSE

In 1994, 45.6 percent of high school seniors had used an illegal drug at least once in their lifetime.

General Information/Advocacy Groups

National Addiction Referral Service
   5900 N. Granite Reef Rd., Suite 105
   Scottsdale, AZ 85250
   (800) 999-8731

National Clearinghouse for Alcohol and Drug Information
   P.O. Box 2345
   Rockville, MD 20847-2345
   (800) 729-6686
   Main source for federal substance abuse information on prevention, education, research, treatment and rehabilitation; NCADI disseminates free publications, posters, videos and audiotapes. Literature searches also are available as well as on-line service and a publication catalog.

National Women's Resource Center for the Prevention of Alcohol, Tobacco, and Other Drugs and Mental Illness
   515 King St., Suite 410
   Alexandria, VA 22314
   (800) 354-8824
   (703) 684-6048 (Fax)
   Sponsored by Substance Abuse and Mental Health Services Administration (SAMHSA), Center collects, analyzes, and disseminates information on women across the life cycle. It provides an information and referral line, training institutes, and conferences.

Hotlines/Helplines

Alcohol and Drug Abuse Helpline
   (800) 821-4357
   Referrals to local alcohol and drug-dependency units and self-help groups.

Alcohol and Drug Abuse Hotline
   (800) 252-6465

Cocaine Hotline
   (800) COCAINE
   (212) 496-6035 (Fax)

Just Say No International
   (800) 258-2766
   (510) 451-6666 (CA)

Samaritans Behavioral Helpline
   (800) 253-1334

Substance Abuse Hotline
   (800) 284-1248

Self-Help/Support Groups

Cocaine Anonymous World Services
   P.O. Box 2000
   Los Angeles, CA 90049-8000
   (310) 559-5833
   (310) 559-2554 (Fax)
   Although not primarily for youth, local chapters welcome youth members who have been affected by someone else's cocaine use or who are in recovery themselves from cocaine abuse.

Narcotics Anonymous
   World Service Office
   P.O. Box 9999
   Van Nuys, CA 91409
   (818) 773-9999
   (818) 700-7000 (Fax)
   Numerous local chapters offer support to recovering drug addicts and information/referrals for family members or friends of drug addicts.

National Asian Pacific American Families Against Substance Abuse, Inc.
   1887 Maplegate St.
   Monterey Park, CA 91755
   (213) 278-0031
   (213) 278-9078 (Fax)

National Association for the Dually Diagnosed
 110 Prince St.
 Kingston, NY 12401
 (800) 331-5362
 (914) 331-4569 (Fax)

National Federation of Parents for Drug-Free Youth
 11159-B South Town Sq.
 St. Louis, MO 63123
 (314) 845-1933
 Local and state chapters strive for a drug-free future by sharing resources to present the best possible prevention delivery system.

On-Line Information and Services

AHCN: Knowledge BASE: drug abuse and dependence
 http://www.housecall.com/databases/ami/convert/001522.html
 Fact sheet on drug abuse and dependence.

Healthtouch On-Line
 http://www.healthtouch.com
 General resources.

National Families in Action
 http://eureka.his.com/public_html/mentors/icfia.html
 Information on how families can fight against illegal drugs.

National Institute on Alcohol Abuse and Alcoholism
 http://www.southwind.com/ncadd/more.html
 Information resource including fact sheets, advocacy, intervention, etc.

Social Issues Links
 Http://www.uchsc.edu/sn/shrs/Nsocial.html
 General advocacy organizations for children.

EATING DISORDERS/ OBESITY

EATING DISORDERS are characterized by severe disturbances in eating behavior. Such disturbances can lead to setbacks in all areas of functioning as well as delayed and possibly destroyed physical and mental growth. They include:

Anorexia Nervosa
Bulimia Nervosa
Food Avoidance Emotional Disorder
Food Refusal
Selective Eating

General Information/Advocacy Groups

American Anorexia/Bulimia Association, Inc.
 293 Central Park West
 New York, NY 10024
 (212) 501-8351
 National nonprofit organization for the prevention, treatment, and cure of eating disorders. Regular membership fee is $50, professional membership fee is $100 (includes option to be listed on referral list).

Anorexia Nervosa and Related Eating Disorders, Inc.
 P.O. Box 5102
 Eugene, OR 97405
 (541) 344-1144
 Nonprofit organization collects information about eating disorders for distribution through booklets and a monthly newsletter. Membership is $15.

Eating Disorders Awareness and Prevention
 P.O. Box 16282
 Pittsburgh, PA 15242
 (412) 922-5922
 National nonprofit organization dedicated to the primary and secondary prevention of eating disorders.

International Association of Eating Disorders Professionals
 123 NW 13th St., #766
 Boca Raton, FL 33432
 (800) 800-8126

Founded in 1985, mission is developing "competency and training standards in the treatment of eating disorders and to devise and implement a system for certifying qualified persons."

National Association of Anorexia Nervosa and Associated Disorders
P.O. Box 7
Highland Park, IL 60035
(847) 831-3438
Nonprofit educational and self-help organization dedicated to helping those with eating disorders. It works to prevent insurance discrimination against people with eating disorders, is involved in consumer advocacy, and has testified at congressional hearings on the dangers of adolescent dieting and potentially dangerous diet products. It disseminates educational materials and sponsors support groups and family hotline. Referrals to treatment centers and local therapists are provided. Publications are available. Memberships fees are $25 for member; $50 for benefactor; and $100 for partner.

National Eating Disorders Organization
6655 S. Yale Ave.
Tulsa, OK 74136
(918) 481-4044
Formerly the National Anorexic Aid Society, NEDO provides information on all eating disorders and referrals to support groups across the country. Membership fees range from $12 for students and $20 for individuals/families to $1,000-$5,000 for lifetime memberships.

Weight Control Information Network
3405 Olandwood Ct., Suite 203
Olney, MD 20832
(301) 570-2177
National source of information on weight-related nutritional disorders for health professionals and the public, WIN provides literature searches on obesity, weight control, and nutritional disorders.

Hotlines/Helplines

National Association of Anorexia Nervosa and Associated Disorders
(847) 831-3438
Hotline for people who have eating disorders and their families.

National Eating Disorder Hotline and Referral Service
(800) 248-3285

Rader Institute for Adolescent and Adult Treatment of Eating Disorders
(800) 255-1818

Self-Help/Support Groups

American Anorexia/Bulimia Association, Inc.
293 Central Park West
New York, NY 10024
(212) 501-8351
Services include referrals to support groups.

Overeaters Anonymous
P.O. Box 44020
Rio Rancho, NM 87194
(505) 891-2664
Groups and literature for young persons and teens.

Rader Institute for Adolescent and Adult Treatment of Eating Disorders
1663 Sawtelle Blvd.
Los Angeles, CA 90025
(800) 255-1818
(310) 477-7822 (Fax)
National association of anorexia nervosa and associated disorders offers hotlines, counseling, support groups, referrals, advocacy, etc.

On-Line Information and Services

alt.support.eating-disord (newsgroup)
Newsgroup discussing eating disorders.

Healthtouch On-Line
http://www.healthtouch.com
Link to resources about eating disorders.

ENCOPRESIS AND ENURESIS

ENCOPRESIS is characterized by repeated passage of feces into inappropriate places (e.g., clothing or floor) whether involuntary or intentional. Chronological age is at least four years. When the passage is involuntary, it is often related to constipation, impaction, and retention with subsequent overflow. Subtypes include *With Constipation and Overflow Incontinence* and *Without Constipation and Overflow Incontinence.*

ENURESIS is characterized by repeated voiding of urine into bed or clothes (whether involuntary or intentional) and is usually accompanied by the presence of clinically significant distress or impairment in social and/or academic functioning. Diagnosis is not made until the child is five or six years old. Subtypes include *Nocturnal,* defined as the passage of urine only during the night-time sleep; *Diurnal,* defined as the passage of urine during waking hours; and *Nocturnal/Diurnal,* a combination of the two subtypes.

General Information/Advocacy Groups

American Sleep Disorders Association
711 Second St. NE, Suite 200
Washington, DC 20002
(202) 544-7499
Represents physicians who specialize in sleep disorder medicine and provides written/verbal information on sleep. Referrals given to local support groups.

Incontinence Information Center
P.O. Box 9
Minneapolis, MN 55440
(800) 543-9632
Provides information about the causes and treatments of incontinence.

National Enuresis Society
7777 Forest Lane
Dallas, TX 75230-2518
(800) NES-8080
Not-for-profit organization dedicated to building greater awareness and understanding of enuresis, the

society gathers, interprets, and offers information to the public and medical professionals who work with children and their families. Publishes *Bedwetting: Facts & Answers,* a brochure for enuretic children and their families.

Hotlines/Helplines

Help for Incontinent People
(800) BLADDER
(803) 579-7902 (Fax)

Incontinence Information Center
(800) 843-4315

Self-Help/Support Groups

Simon Foundation for Incontinence
P.O. Box 385
Wilmette, IL 60091
(847) 864-3913
Support and advocacy for people suffering from incontinence; 500 groups nationwide.

On-Line INformation and Services

AHCN Knowledge Base: Encopresis
http://www.housecall.com/databases/ami/convert/001570.html
Fact sheet on encopresis.

National Enuresis Society
http://www.peds.umn.edu/centers/NES/
Information and resources on enuresis and encopresis.

Phone Directory
http://www.chmc.org/phonext/clinics/briefs/cli477.htm
Phone numbers to call for information on enuresis/encopresis.

FOSTER FAMILIES

Approximately one of every 226 children in the U.S. is living in a foster home.
—"Children and Foster Homes" by N. McKellar in *Children's Needs: Psychological Perspectives*, National Association of School Psychologists, 1987.

General Information/Advocacy Groups

Child Welfare League of America
  440 First St. NW, Suite 310
  Washington, DC 20001-2085
  (202) 638-2952
  (202) 638-4004 (Fax)
  National consortium of numerous organizations offers information, support, and referrals related to: abused and neglected children and their families, family preservation, child care, foster care, adoption, residential group homes, teens who are parents or pregnant. Child Welfare League offers a wide array of publications on these issues.

National Foster Care Resource Center
  Eastern Michigan University
  102 King Hall
  Ypsilanti, MI 48197
  (313) 487-0374
  Publishes and distributes 20 publications in the Foster Parent Education Series.

Hotlines/Helplines

Orphan Foundation of America
  (800) 950-4673

On-Line Information and Services

Comprehensive Plan for 1995-97
  http://www.ordata.com/~newmant/children
  Lane County Commission on Children and Families. Promotes the wellness of children and families. Links to resources on foster care, juvenile reform/youth development and child resiliency.

Foster Care and Adoption Assistance
  http://www.acf.dhhs.gov/ACFPrograms/FosterCare/foster.htm
  Fact sheet.

Michigan Foster and Adoptive Parents Network
  http://www.grnet.com/mfapa/index.html

New Hampshire Foster Parent Home Page
  http://top.monad.net/~nhfpa/

GIFTEDNESS

Gifted children often feel "different" from their peers, which can lead to feelings of isolation, loneliness and inadequate social interactions.
—"Children and Giftedness" by B. Gridley and S. Gatten in *Helping Children Grow Up in the '90s*, National Association of School Psychologists, 1992.

General Information/Advocacy Groups

American Association for Gifted Children
1121 W. Main St., Suite 100
Durham, NC 27701
(919) 683-1400

Association for High-Potential Children (AHPC)
P.O. Box 1344
Eau Claire, WI 54702
(715) 833-8454

Creative Education Foundation
1050 Union Rd.
Buffalo, NY 14224
(716) 675-3181

Educational Resources Information Center
Clearinghouse on Disabilities and Gifted Children
Council for Exceptional Children
1920 Association Dr.
Reston, VA 22091-1589
(800) 328-0272
Provides information and referrals on topics related to the education of disabled and gifted children. It provides materials on all aspects of special education, including IDEA, IEP, and the ADA and also has bibliographies, materials for parents and teachers, and newsletters.

Gifted Child Society, Inc.
190 Rock Rd.
Glen Rock, NJ 07452
(201) 444-6530

National Association for Creative Children and Adults
8080 Springvalley Dr.
Cincinnati, OH 45236
(513) 631-1777

National Association for Gifted Children
1707 I St. NW, Suite 550
Washington, DC 20036
(202) 785-4268

National Association of Private Schools for Exceptional Children
1522 K St. NW, Suite 1032
Washington, DC 20005
(202) 408-3338
Provides referrals to private special education programs.

Supporting Emotional Needs of the Gifted
Kent State University
405 White Hall
Kent, OH 44243
(330) 672-2294

World Council for Gifted and Talented Children
P.O. Box 218
Teacher's College
Columbia University
525 W. 120th St.
New York, NY 10027
(212) 678-3851

Self-Help/Support Groups

American Mensa, Ltd.
201 Main St., Suite 1101
Fort Worth, TX 76102
(800) 666-3672
(817) 332-7299 (Fax)
70107.2242 CompuServe (e-mail)
Although primarily an organization for adults, many local chapters have special activities/programs for youth.

National Beta Club
151 W. Lee St.
P.O. Box 730
Spartanburg, SC 29304
(800) 845-8281
(803) 542-9300 (Fax)
For children in grades 5-12, an academic, leadership, and service organization for outstanding youth.

National Junior Honor Society
National Association of Secondary Principals
1904 Association Dr.
Reston, VA 22091
(703) 860-0200
(703) 476-5432 (Fax)
For youth who are outstanding in scholarship, leadership, character, and service.

On-Line Information and Services

ERIC Digests on Gifted Education
http://buerkle.arc.leon.k12.fl.us/ericgifted.html

Gifted and Talented Resources Home Page
http://www.eskimo.com/~user/kids.html
Resources for talented and gifted children.

National Association for Gifted Children
http://www.rmplc.co.uk/eduweb/sites/nagc/research.ht
ml
Research on programs for gifted children.

Special Needs Education Network (SNE)
http://schoolnet2.carelton.ca/sne/gedsites.html
Links to pages with resources on support for gifted children.

LEARNING DIFFERENCES/ SPECIAL EDUCATION

The common denominator of special education students is that they have educational needs significantly different from those of most regular education students of their age, to the extent that specialized instruction is necessary to help them learn commensurate with their abilities. Special education students cannot learn effectively in their area of special need when instructed with regular education methods and materials.
—K. Shore. *The Special Education Handbook. New York: Warner Books, 1986.*

General Information/Advocacy Groups

ENABLEDATA
8455 Colesville Rd., Suite 935
Silver Spring, MD 20910
(800) 227-0216
Maintains a database on assistive technology devices for people with disabilities.

American Academy of Pediatrics
141 Northwest Point Blvd.
Elk Grove Village, IL 60009
(800) 433-9016
Provides two pamphlets: "Learning Disabilities and Children" and "Learning Disabilities and Young Adults."

Association for Children and Adults with Learning Disabilities
4156 Library Rd.
Pittsburgh, PA 15234
(412) 341-1515

Association for Individually Guided Education
Hutchinson United School District - 308
P.O. Box 1908
Hutchinson, KS 67504
(316) 665-4400

Association of Educational Therapists
P.O. Box 946
14852 Ventura Blvd.
Sherman Oaks, CA 91365
(818) 380-6895
National professional association for practitioners combining special education skills and counseling.

Child Find
25 Industrial Park Rd.
Middletown, CT 06457
(800) 842-3678
Operated by the Special Education Resource Center and directed by the State Dept. of Education dedicated to identifying, evaluating, and placing all unidentified/unserved students with disabilities.

Clearinghouse for Specialized Media and Technology
P.O. Box 944272
Sacramento, CA 94244
(916) 445-5103
Provides resource materials for people working with students with disabilities.

Clearinghouse on Disability Information
330 C St. SW, Room 3132
Washington, DC 20202-2524
(202) 205-8241

College Project at the Center for Psychiatric Rehabilitation
930 Commonwealth Ave.
Boston, MA 02215
(617) 353-3549
(617) 353-7700 (Fax)
Conducts research, develops educational materials, disseminates new knowledge, and provides training and program consultation in the area of psychiatric rehabilitation. A catalog of materials is available.

Disabled Reader Group
International Reading Association
800 Barksdale Rd.
P.O. Box 8139
McMurray, PA 15137
(302) 731-1600
Dedicated to increasing awareness of reading disabilities, improving the quality of educational programs, and promoting interdisciplinary cooperation and understanding around learning disabilities.

Educational Referral Service
2222 Eastlake Ave. E.
Seattle, WA 98102
(206) 323-1838
Specializes in helping match children with disabilities with appropriate educational programs and services.

Educational Resources Information Center
Clearinghouse on Disabilities and Gifted Children
Council for Exceptional Children
1920 Association Dr.
Reston, VA 22091-1589
(800) 328-0272
Provides information and referrals on topics related to the education of disabled and gifted children and materials on all aspects of special education, including IDEA, IEP, and the ADA. Bibliographies, materials for parents and teachers, and newsletters are available.

Institute for Research in Learning Disabilities
University of Kansas
3060 Robert J. Dole
Lawrence, KS 66045
(913) 864-4780
Provides information on research findings about learning disabilities, especially in children.

International Council for Learning Disabilities
National Office
P.O. Box 40303
Overland Park, KS 66204
(913) 492-8755
Fosters information exchange among professionals working with people with learning disabilities.

Learning Disabilities Association of America
4156 Library Rd.
Pittsburgh, PA 15234
(412) 341-1515
Concerned parents devoted to defining and finding solutions for the broad spectrum of learning problems offer numerous publications and a video rental service. Association has 50 state affiliates and over 775 local chapters.

National Association of Private Schools for Exceptional Children
1522 K St. NW, Suite 1032
Washington, DC 20005
(202) 408-3338
Provides referrals to private special education programs.

National Center for Learning Disabilities
381 Park Ave. South
New York, NY 10016
(212) 545-7510
(212) 545-9665 (Fax)
Provides a national information and referral service, publications, advocacy, and educational programs.

National Center for School Based Health Information Systems
Children's Hospital
1056 East 19th Ave.
Denver, CO 80218
(303) 922-5370

National Center for Youth with Disabilities
University of Minnesota
420 Delaware St. SE
Minneapolis, MN 55455
(612) 626-2825
(612) 626-2134 (Fax)
(612) 624-3939 (TTY)
ncyd@gold.tc.umn.edu (e-mail)
http://www.peds.umn.edu.centers (Web-site)
Provides information, resources, and policy advocacy for youth with chronic disabilities or illnesses; runs the National Resource Library database through its toll-free number.

National Clearinghouse on Postsecondary Education for People with Disabilities
One Dupont Circle, Suite 800
Washington, DC 20036-1193
(800) 544-3284
heath@acnche.edu (e-mail)

National Data Bank for Disabled Student Services
University of Maryland
Shoemaker Bldg., Room 0126
College Park, MD 20742
(301) 314-7682
Helps people access statistics related to students with disabilities and the services provided for them throughout the U.S.

National Information Center for Children and Youth with Disabilities
P.O. Box 1492
Washington, DC 20013
(800) 695-0285
(703) 893-8614 (Fax)
Provides information and referral services, publications, and technical assistance to families and practitioners. Numerous free publications are available as well as other information on topics such as early intervention, special education, transition planning, state resource guides, and numerous other specific disabilities.

Office of Special Education and Rehabilitative Services
U.S. Dept. of Education
330 C St. SW, Room 3132
Washington, DC 20202-2524
(202) 205-8241
Provides leadership to achieve full integration and participation in society of people with disabilities by ensuring equal opportunity and access to and excellence in education, employment, and community living. OSERS is divided into three program areas: Office of Special Education, Rehabilitative Services Administration, and National Institute on Disability and Rehabilitation Research.

Orton Dyslexia Society
Chester Bldg., Suite 380
8600 LaSalle Rd.
Baltimore, MD 21286-2044
(410) 296-0232
Information for people with dyslexia.

Hotlines/Helplines

American Disability Association Helpline
   (800) 669-3362

Americans with Disabilities Act Information Line
   (800) 514-0301
   (800) 514-0383 (TDD)

National Association for the Education of Young
Children
   (800) 424-2460

National Clearinghouse for Bilingual Education
   (800) 321-6223

Orton Dyslexia Society
   (800) ABCD-123

Self-Help/Support Groups

Access Ability Resource Center
   1056 East 19th Ave.
   P.O. Box 410
   Denver, CO 80218
   (303) 861-6250
   (303) 861-6411 (Fax)
   Provides evaluation, information, and support to
   families of children with learning disabilities.

Federation for Children with Special Needs
   95 Berkeley St., Suite 104
   Boston, MA 02173
   (617) 482-2915 or (800) 331-0688
   (617) 695-2935 (Fax)
   Coalition of parent groups offering a variety of services
   to parents of children with varying disabilities.

Learning Disabilities Network
   72 Sharp St. Suite A-2
   Hingham, MA 02043
   (617) 340-5605
   Nonprofit organization provides educational and support services to people with learning disabilities, their
   families, and practitioners.

MATRIX, a Parent Network and Resource Center
   320 Nova Albion Way
   San Rafael, CA 94903
   (415) 499-3877
   Support, information, and resource center for parents
   who have discovered their child has a disability or special need. Support is offered by parents who have
   gone through a similar process.

National Parent Network on Disabilities
   1600 Prince St., Suite 115
   Alexandria, VA 22314
   (703) 684-6763
   (703) 548-6191 (Fax)
   Coalition of parents and parent groups who advocate
   for the rights of people with disabilities.

TASK (Team of Advocates for Special Kids)
   100 West Cerritos
   Anaheim, CA 92805
   (714) 533-TASK
   Provides services, information, support, training, legal
   information, advocacy, workshops, and referrals for
   families of children with disabilities. Provides specialized services to disabled children of Vietnam Veterans.

Young Adult Institute and Workshop
   460 W. 34th St., 11th Floor
   New York, NY 10001
   (212) 563-7474
   Programs enable persons with mental retardation,
   learning disabilities, or emotional illness to progress
   toward a more "normal" life.

On-Line Information and Services

Disabilities Resource Page
   http://www.valdosta.peachnet.edu/vsu/dept/coe/coed/s
   ped/camp/special/disable.html

Resources for Research on Disabilities (includes technology section)
   http://www.sped.ukans.edu/speddisabilitiesstuff/wel-
   come.htm/

MEDICATION/ PSYCHOPHARMACOLOGY

Recent surveys estimate that over 2,000,000 children in the U.S. are taking Ritalin, four times as many as in any other country.

General Information/Advocacy Groups

Child Psychopharmacology Information Center
  University of Wisconsin
  Dept. of Psychiatry
  600 Highland Ave.
  Madison, WI 53792
  (608) 263-6171

Food and Drug Administration
  Office of Consumer Affairs
  5600 Fishers Lane, HFE-50
  Rockville, MD 20857
  (301) 443-3170

Lithium Information Center
  Dean Foundation
  800 Excelsior Dr., Suite 302
  Madison, WI 53717-1914
  (608) 836-8070
  Provides biomedical and general information about lithium and other treatments for bipolar (manic-depressive) disorder; offers referrals to local medical professionals and support groups. Written materials are available for a fee.

Office of Alternative Medicine
  National Institutes of Health
  9000 Rockville Pk., Bldg. 31, Room 5B-38
  Mail Stop 2182
  Bethesda, MD 20892
  (301) 402-2466

U.S. Pharmacopeia
  12601 Twinbrook Pkwy.
  Rockville, MD 20852
  (800) 877-6733
  Establishes standards for the use of medicines and related items and publishes drug standards publications, drug information publications, and patient edu-

cation materials. Through a partnership with the FDA, the USP maintains a drug reporting program through which providers can report medication errors, safety concerns, observations, or any problem concerning drug quality or administration. Brochures are available for many antidepressants, antidyskinetics, antianxiety, and antipsychotic medications.

Hotlines/Helplines

Paxil Access to Care Program
  (800) 729-4544
  Provides eligible consumers with free or low-cost supplies of the antidepressant medication Paxil.

Risperdal Helpline
  Jannsen Pharmaceutica
  (800) 676-6225
  A 24-hour helpline sponsored by the manufacturer of the anti-psychotic drug Risperdal. Consumers and professionals can obtain information on drug therapy.

On-Line Information and Services

Medicine on Line
  http://vega.crbm.cnrs-mop.fr/bioscience/medinfo/med-info.htm

Psychotherapeutic Drugs
  http://www.onlinepsych.com/treat/drugs.htm
  Information on typical medication prescribed for mental health conditions.

Searchable Database on Pharmacology
  http://krscience.dialog.com/ScienceBase/Forms/Pharmacology.html

MENTAL RETARDATION

The essential feature of **MENTAL RETARDATION** is subnormal intellectual development or functioning that is the result of congenital causes, brain injury, or disease. It is characterized by any of various deficiencies, ranging from impaired learning ability to social and vocational inadequacy.

General Information/Advocacy Groups

American Association on Mental Retardation
171 Kalorama Rd. NW
Washington, DC 20009
(800) 424-3688
Information on legal rights, services, and facilities for mentally retarded persons.

Association for Retarded Citizens
P.O. Box 1047
Arlington, TX 76004
(817) 261-6003

Council for Exceptional Children
1920 Association Dr.
Reston, VA 22091
(703) 620-3660
Goal is to improve availability/quality of education for disabled and gifted children.

Federation for Children with Special Needs
312 Stuart St., 2nd Fl.
Boston, MA 02116
(617) 482-2915

Mental Retardation Association of America
211 E. 300 South, Suite 212
Salt Lake City, UT 84111
(801) 328-1575

Hotlines/Helplines

National Fragile X Foundation
(800) 688-8765
(303) 333-6155
(303) 333-4369 (Fax)

Self-Help/Support Groups

Young Adult Institute and Workshop
460 W. 34th St., 11th Floor
New York, NY 10001
(212) 563-7474
Programs enable persons with mental retardation, learning disabilities, or emotional illness to progress toward a more "normal" life.

On-Line Information and Services

Protection and Advocacy
http://metronet.com/~thearc/posits/pa.html
Information about advocacy organization.

Facts about Mental Retardation
http://www.gate.net/~bestbud/facts.html

TRFN - Mental Health
http://trfn.pgh.pa.us/health/mental.html
Parent and child guidance center.

Self-Advocacy Groups
http://metronet.com/~thearc/posits/selfadv.html

OBSESSIVE-COMPULSIVE DISORDER

The essential features of OBSESSIVE-COMPULSIVE DISORDER are recurrent obsessions or compulsions (i.e., fear of dirt or germs, a need for symmetry and order, preoccupations with objects) that are severe enough to be time-consuming or cause marked distress or significant impairment. Rituals (i.e., grooming, touching, repeating, ordering, counting) are the deliberate and repeated behaviors that an OCD child will use to relieve the anxiety caused by obsessive thoughts.

General Information/Advocacy Groups

Anxiety Disorders Association of America
600 Executive Blvd.
Rockville, MD 20852
(301) 231-9350
(301) 231-7392 (Fax)
Provides an information and referral service to help identify treatment facilities, local self-help groups and offers publications and membership information. A list of professionals in each state is available for $3. Call (900) 737-3400 ($2/minute) for information on professional treatment, local self-help groups, publications, and membership.

Obsessive Compulsive Information Center
Dean Foundation
800 Excelsior Dr., #302
Madison, WI 53717
(608) 836-8070
Collects and disseminates information about obsessive compulsive and related disorders such as trichotillo-mania (hair pulling), body dysmorphic disorder, and hypochondriasis; provides bibliographies and copies of some articles and make referrals to physicians and support groups. Publishes *Obsessive Compulsive Disorder: A Guide.*

OC Foundation, Inc.
P.O. Box 70
Milford, CT 06460
(203) 878-5669
(203)874-3843 (Info Line)

jphs28a@prodigy.com (e-mail)
Volunteer nonprofit organization dedicated to improving the welfare of people with OCD through education, research, and services provided to people with obsessive compulsive disorder, their families, and concerned professionals. Basic membership fee is $30 per year and entitles members to discounts on literature. Publications include: *OCD Newsletter* (bimonthly), *Kidscope* (newsletter for children with OCD), and *Learning to Live with Obsessive Compulsive Disorder* (2nd ed.).

Self-Help/Support Groups

Obsessive-Compulsive Anonymous
P.O. Box 215
New Hyde Park, NY 11040
(516) 741-4901
12-step self-help group for people with OCD; 50 groups nationwide.

On-Line Information and Services

Children Now (advocacy organization)
http://www.dnai.com/~children/
Information about organization's advocacy programs.

KidsSource
http://www.kidsource.com/kidscource/content/obsess.html
Place where kids can get information and communicate with each other about OCD.

PAIN MANAGEMENT

It is estimated that 10 to 20 percent of all children have a chronic medical disorder. Two percent of all children suffer from a severe chronic illness that regularly interferes with daily activities.

—"Children and Chronic Illness" by M. Potter in *Children's Needs: Psychological Perspectives*, National Association of School Psychologists, 1987.

General Information/Advocacy Groups

American Association for the Study of Headache
875 Kings Hwy., Suite 200
Woodbury, NJ 08096
(609) 845-0322

Information Exchange on Young Adult Chronic Patients
20 Squadron Blvd., Suite 400
New City, NY 10956
(914) 634-0050
Gathers and disseminates information about treatment programs/methods for persons who have needed mental health services for at least two years.

National Headache Foundation
5252 N. Western Ave.
Chicago, IL 60625
(800) 843-2256

Hotlines/Helplines

National Head Injury Foundation Family Helpline
(800) 444-6443
(202) 296-8850 (Fax)
Provides information and resources for people with head injury, their families, and the professionals who provide rehabilitative care; offers educational material on the impact of a brain injury, location of rehabilitative facilities, and availability of community services; promotes activities related to the prevention of head injuries.

Self-Help/Support Groups

American Chronic Pain Association
P.O. Box 850
Rocklin, CA 95677
(916) 632-0922
Network of 800 chapters worldwide.

American Pain Society
P.O. Box 468
Des Plaines, IL 60016-0468
(847) 966-5595

National Chronic Pain Outreach Association
4922 Hampden Lane
Bethesda, MD 20814
(301) 652-4948
Maintains a database of support groups by state.

National Parent to Parent Support and Information System
P.O. Box 907
Blue Ridge, GA 30513
(800) 651-1151
Links parents of children with rare disorders or special health care needs.

On-Line Information and Services

Monitoring the Quality of Pain Management
http://www.stat.washington.edu/TALARIA/LS8.0.html

Pediatric Pain Mailing List Announcement
http://neurosurgery.mgh.harvard.edu/pedipain.htm

Pediatric Pain Management
http://www.icsi.net/medical/ped.html

PERVASIVE DEVELOPMENTAL DISORDERS

PERVASIVE DEVELOPMENTAL DISORDERS include:

Asperger's Disorder
Autism (see also separate section)
Childhood Disintegrative Disorder
Fragile X Syndrome
Pervasive Developmental Disorder Not Otherwise
   Specified (including Atypical Autism)
Rett's Disorder

General Information/Advocacy Groups

IRSA (International Rett Syndrome Association)
   9121 Piscataway Rd., #2B
   Clinton, MD 20735-2561
   (800) 818-RETT
   For parents, professionals and others concerned with
   Rett syndrome, IRSA provides information and referral, peer support among parents, and encourages
   research.

National Fragile X Foundation
   1441 York St., #215
   Denver, CO 80206
   (800) 688-8765
   Makes available information to promote education and
   research regarding Fragile X syndrome; provides
   phone support, newsletter, information and referrals.

Self-Help/Support Groups

Federation for Children with Special Needs
   95 Berkeley St., Suite 104
   Boston, MA 02173
   (617) 482-2915 or (800) 331-0688
   (617) 695-2935 (Fax)
   Coalition of parent groups offering a variety of services
   to parents of children with varying disabilities.

On-Line Information and Services

Development Disorders Page
   http://www.option.org/s_s02.html

Developmental Disabilities Facilities
   http://www.bergen.com/health/db/listde.html
   Links to resources on developmental disorders.

Monitoring the Quality of Pain Management
   http://www.stat.washington.edu/TALARIA/LS8.0.html
   Suggestions for professionals.

POST TRAUMATIC STRESS DISORDER

The essential feature of **POST TRAUMATIC STRESS DISORDER** is the development of characteristic symptoms following exposure to an extremely traumatic stressor involving personal experience of an event that involves actual or threatened death or serious injury or other threat to one's physical integrity; or witnessing an event that involves death, injury, or a threat to the physical integrity of another person; or learning about unexpected or violent death, serious harm, or threat of death or injury experienced by a family member or other close associate.

General Information/Advocacy Groups

International Society for Traumatic Stress Study
60 Revere Dr., Suite 500
Northbrook, IL 60002
(847) 480-9028

National Center for Post Traumatic Stress Disorder
VA Medical and Regional Office Center (116D)
White River Junction, VT 05009
(802) 296-5132

Sidran Foundation
2328 W. Joppa Rd., Suite 15
Lutherville, MD 21093
(410) 825-8888
sidran@access.digex.net (e-mail)
Provides information and advocates in support of people who have experienced trauma and have trauma-related disorders. Develops public education workshops on the psychological outcomes of severe childhood trauma for adult survivors, partners, caregivers, and professionals. Publishes books and educational materials on traumatic stress disorders, dissociative disorders, child sexual abuse, ritual abuse, self-injury, and self-help/recovery.

Self-Help/Support Groups

Anxiety Disorders Association of America
600 Executive Blvd.
Rockville, MD 20852
(301) 231-9350
(301) 231-7392 (Fax)
Provides an information and referral service to help identify treatment facilities, local self-help groups and offers publications and membership information. A list of professionals in each state is available for $3. Call (900) 737-3400 ($2/minute) for information on professional treatment, local self-help groups, publications, and membership.

On-Line Information and Services

Post Traumatic Stress Resources
http://www.long-beach.va.gov/lbec/ptsd.html
Links to helpful pages

Mental Health Guide
http://www.cmhc.com/guide/trauma.htm
Resources on stress and trauma.

RUNAWAYS AND MISSING CHILDREN

Each year in the U.S., approximately one million children run away from home.
—"Children and Running Away" by J. Deni in *Children's Needs: Psychological Perspectives*, National Association of School Psychologists, 1987.

General Information/Advocacy Groups

Homelessness Information Exchange
1612 K St. NW, Suite 1004
Washington, DC 20006
(202) 775-1322
(202) 775-1316 (Fax)

National Center for Missing and Exploited Children
2101 Wilson Blvd., Suite 550
Arlington, VA 22201-3052
(703) 235-3900
Provides assistance to parents and law enforcement agencies in locating missing children and preventing child exploitation.

National Clearinghouse on Runaway and Homeless Youth
P.O. Box 13505
Silver Spring, MD 20911-3505
(301) 608-8098

National Resource Center on Homelessness and Mental Illness
262 Delaware Ave.
Delmar, NY 12054
(800) 444-7415
(518) 439-7612 (Fax)

Hotlines/Helplines

Boys Town National Hotline
(800) 448-3000
Hotline for children/adolescents who are runaways, experiencing abuse, or contemplating suicide.

Childhelp USA
1345 North Elcentro Ave.
Hollywood, CA 90028
(800) 422-4453
Hotline for children/adolescents who are runaways, experiencing abuse, or contemplating suicide; also handles calls from parents.

Home Run National Runaway Hotline
(800) HIT-HOME
Referrals to shelters, counseling, message service for children and parents.

National Center for Missing and Exploited Children
(800) 843-5678

National Runaway Switchboard
(800) 621-4000
Free and confidential 24-hour crisis intervention for teens and their families; conference calls among teens, parents, and appropriate agencies.

Runaway Hotline
(800) 231-6946
Hotline for child/adolescent runaways; provides confidential relay of messages from youths to parents without revealing locations.

Youth Crisis Hotline
(800) 448-4663
Hotline for children/adolescents who are runaways, experiencing abuse, or contemplating suicide.

Self-Help/Support Groups

NAMI Homeless and Missing Service
1239C Russell Pkwy., Suite 20
Warner Robbins, GA 31088
(912) 328-3555
National Alliance for the Mentally Ill sponsors the Missing Persons Service to help locate homeless or missing persons with mental illness. Emergency hotline gives support to families and works with them to find the missing person.

On-Line Information and Services

Homeless Missing Person Project
  http://www.inca.net/hmpp/press.html
  Resources for locating missing children.

SEXUAL ABUSE AND INCEST

A 1992 study by the National Committee for Prevention of Child Abuse showed that nearly three million U.S. children were reported as suspected victims during that year. An estimated one of every three girls and one of every seven boys in the U.S. will be sexually abused before age 18.

General Information/Advocacy Groups

Alternatives to Sexual Abuse
  P.O. Box 25537
  Portland, OR 97229
  (503) 644-6600

American Association for Protecting Children
  c/o American Humane Association
  63 Inverness Dr. E.
  Englewood, CO 80112-5117
  (303) 792-9900

Center for Child Protection
  Children's Hospital
  3020 Children's Way
  San Diego, CA 92132
  (619) 974-8017

Center for the Prevention of Sexual and Domestic Violence
  936 N. 34th St., Suite 200
  Seattle, WA 98103
  (206) 634-1903
  (206) 634-0115 (Fax)
  cpsdv@cpsdv.seanet.com (e-mail)
  Educational resource center on sexual and domestic violence issues and clergy abuse works to train and educate clergy and lay people to recognize domestic violence and to support the victims. Publications are available.

Children's Rights Council
  220 I St. NE, Suite 230
  Washington, DC 20002
  (202) 547-6227

Family Violence and Sexual Assault Institute
1310 Clinic Dr.
Tyler, TX 75701
(903) 595-6600

National Coalition Against Sexual Assault
912 N. 2nd St.
Harrisburg, PA
(717) 232-7460

National Committee for Prevention of Child Abuse
332 S. Michigan Ave., Suite 1600
Chicago, IL 60604-4357
(312) 663-3520

National Resource Center on Child Sexual Abuse
2204 Whitesburg Dr., Suite 200
Huntsville, AL 35801
(205) 534-6868
(800) 543-7006 (Hotline)
Provides technical support to all professionals who work with sexually abused children and their families. Training opportunities include comprehensive child sexual abuse intervention training, national symposium on child sexual abuse, and teleseminars. Also offers referrals for treatment and consultation and reference library, information papers, and national directory of child sexual abuse treatment programs (a current, annotated listing of approximately 850 programs in the U.S. and its territories - cost is $25 plus $3.50 postage), monographs, and program and practice briefs.

Safer Society Program and Press
P.O. Box 340
Brandon, VT 05733
(802) 247-3132 or (802) 247-5141
Information and referral service for both sexual abuse victims and offenders maintains a nationwide database of specialized child, juvenile, and adult sex offender and victim treatment programs. Publications are available for professionals, victims, and offenders.

Society's League Against Molestation
Women Against Rape/Childwatch
P.O. Box 346
Dollingswood, NJ 08108
(609) 858-7800

Sidran Foundation
2328 W. Joppa Rd., Suite 15
Lutherville, MD 21093
(410) 825-8888
sidran@access.digex.net (e-mail)
Provides information and advocates in support of people who have experienced trauma and have trauma-related disorders. Develops public education workshops on the psychological outcomes of severe childhood trauma for adult survivors, partners, caregivers, and professionals. Publishes books and educational materials on traumatic stress disorders, dissociative disorders, child sexual abuse, ritual abuse, self-injury, and self-help/recovery.

Hotlines/Helplines

National Child Abuse Hotline
(800) 422-4453
Crisis hotline for children and adolescents experiencing abuse.

National Resource Center on Child Sexual Abuse
(800) 543-7006

Parents Anonymous
(800) 421-0353
Helpline for parents who fear they may abuse their children.

Rape, Abuse, and Incest National Network (RAINN)
(800) 656-4673
24-hour, 7-day-a-week hotline for victims of sexual assault automatically connects callers to a rape crisis center in their community where they can receive counseling and support.

Youth Crisis Hotline
(800) 448-4663
Hotline for children/adolescents who are runaways, experiencing abuse, or contemplating suicide.

Self-Help/Support Groups

Daughters and Sons United
  Giaretto Institute
  232 E. Gish Rd., First Floor
  San Jose, CA 95112
  (408) 453-7611, ext. 1229
  (408) 453-9064 (Fax)
  Over 100 local chapters offer information, counseling, and resources for children who have been or are being sexually abused.

Parents United International, Inc.
  615 15th St.
  Modesto, CA 95354-2510
  (202) 573-3446
  Provides treatment for child sexual abuse; offers groups for perpetrators, victims, and family members; has over 70 chapters nationwide.

On-Line Information and Services

Sexual abuse resources for boys of abuse/incest
  http://www.crl.com/~the fly/abuse/sexualabuse.html

Victims of Incest Can Emerge Survivors (VOICES) in Action Inc.
  http://www.cs.utk.edu/~bartley/other/VOICES.html
  Information on how this organization can help you.

SEXUAL IDENTITY/ CONCERNS

Homosexuality in children and adolescents has been relatively ignored by the professional literature, yet more and more students are identifying themselves as gay and are seeking help in understanding their homosexuality.
  —"Children and Homosexuality" by D. Canaday in *Children's Needs: Psychological Perspectives,* National Association of School Psychologists, 1987.

General Information/Advocacy Groups

Parents, Families and Friends of Lesbians and Gays
  1101 14th St. NW, Suite 1030
  Washington, DC 20005
  (202) 638-4200
  (202) 638-0243 (Fax)
  pflagntl@aol.com (e-mail)
  Numerous local chapters provide information, resources, publications, and support to family and friends of people who are lesbian, gay, or bisexual. Hosts an annual national conference for gay, lesbian, and bisexual people and their family and friends.

Hotlines/Helplines

Gay/Lesbian/Bisexual Youth Hotline
  Indianapolis Youth Group
  P.O. Box 20716
  Indianapolis, IN 46220-0716
  (800) 347-8336(TEEN)
  (317) 541-8726
  (317) 545-8594 (Fax)
  Provides an information and support hotline to youth who have identified themselves as gay/lesbian or bisexual; staffed Friday through Sunday from 7:00 p.m. to midnight, and Monday through Thursday from 7:00 p.m. to 10:00 p.m. (EST).

Homosexuals Anonymous Fellowship Services
  Support for people who experience unwanted homosexual feelings.
  (800) 288-HAFS

Pride Institute for Lesbian and Gay Mental Health Foundation helps its constituency who have chemical dependency and mental health issues.
(800) 54-PRIDE

Self-Help/Support Groups

Children of Lesbian and Gays Everywhere (COLAGE)
2300 Market St.
P.O. Box 165
San Francisco, CA 94114
(415) 861-KIDS

Parents and Friends of Lesbians and Gays (P-FLAG)
P.O. Box 20308
Denver, CO 80220
(303) 333-0286
Support group for parents, with local chapters in many cities. Publishes *Now That You Know: What Every Parent Should Know About Homosexuality,* a book that discusses parents' views of their children's homosexuality while giving information about homosexuality and issues surrounding it.

Parents, Families and Friends of Lesbians and Gays
1101 14th St. NW, Suite 1030
Washington, DC 20005
(202) 638-4200
(202) 638-0243 (Fax)
pflagntl@aol.com (e-mail)
Numerous local chapters provide information, resources, publications, and support to family and friends of people who are lesbian, gay, or bisexual. Hosts an annual national conference for gay, lesbian, and bisexual people and their family and friends.

On-Line Information and Services

Gay and Lesbian Parents Coalition International
http://qrd.tcp.com/qrd/orgs/GLPCI/on-line.info
Provides advocacy and support.

Helping Hands
http://www.sfbayguardian.com/Epicenter/96_06/062696gpfam.html
Information on where to find resources on sexual identity concerns.

SLEEP DISORDERS

Primary **SLEEP DISORDERS** are subdivided into *dyssomnias,* characterized by abnormalities in the amount, quality, or timing of sleep, and *parasomnias,* characterized by abnormal behavior or physiological events occurring in association with sleep, specific sleep stages, or sleep-wake transitions.

General Information/Advocacy Groups

American Sleep Disorders Association
  711 Second St. NE, Suite 200
  Washington, DC 20002
  (202) 544-7499
  Represents physicians who specialize in sleep disorder medicine and provides written/verbal information on sleep. Referrals given to local support groups.

Self-Help/Support Groups

American Sleep Disorders Association
  711 Second St. NE Suite 200
  Washington, DC 20002
  (202) 544-7499
  Referrals given to local support groups.

Narcolepsy Network
  P.O. Box 1365, FDR Station
  New York, NY 10150
  (914) 834-2855 (East)
  (415) 591-7884 (West)
  Support and education for persons with narcolepsy and other sleep disorders and their families; helps with coping skills, family, and community problems; has 100 national groups.

On-Line Information and Services

Northside Hospital Sleep Disorders Center
  http://www.nshsleep.com/

Sleepnet - Links to other sleep disorder sites
  http://www.sleepnet.com/links.htm

STEPFAMILIES

It is estimated that one in five children will live in a stepfamily. Less than 25 percent of all homes are composed of the biological unit of mother, father, and their offspring.
  —"Children and Stepfamilies" by S. Kupisch in *Children's Needs: Psychological Perspectives,* National Association of School Psychologists, 1987.

General Information/Advocacy Groups

Stepfamily Association of America
  215 Centennial Mall, #212
  Lincoln, NE 68508-1814
  (800) 735-0329
  Offers information and advocacy for stepfamilies.

Stepfamily Association of Illinois, Inc.
  P.O. Box 3124
  Oak Park, IL 60303
  (708) 848-0909

Stepfamily Foundation
  333 West End Ave.
  New York, NY 10023
  (212) 877-3244
  (212) 362-7030 (Fax)
  (212) 799-STEP (24 Hour Info)

Hotlines/Helplines

Stepfamily Foundation
  (212) 744-6924

Self-Help/Support Groups

Stepfamily Association of America
  215 Centennial Mall, #212
  Lincoln, NE 68508-1814
  (800) 735-0329
  Provides self-help programs through 70 local chapters nationwide.

On-Line Information and Services

Stepfamily Solution
http://www.publiccom.com/web/stepkid
Web page offering information and resources.

Parents Place
http://www.parentsplace.com
Help for parents on how to deal with stepfamilies.

STRESS DISORDERS

The essential feature of **Acute Stress Disorder** is the development of characteristic anxiety, dissociative, and other symptoms that occurs within one month of exposure to an extremely traumatic stressor. Symptoms of despair and hopelessness may be expected and may be sufficiently severe and persistent to meet criteria for a Major Depressive Episode.

General Information/Advocacy Groups

American Institute on Stress
124 Park Ave.
Yonkers, NY 10703
(800) 247-3529
(914) 965-6267 (Fax)
stress124@earthlink.net (e-mail)
National service acts as an educational clearinghouse of information relating to stress.

Center for Anxiety and Stress Treatment
4350 Executive Dr., Suite 204
San Diego, CA 92121
(619) 542-0536
(619) 542-0730 (Fax)

International Society for the Study of Multiple Personality Disorder and Dissociation
5700 Old Orchard Rd.
Skokie, IL 60077
(708) 966-4322

International Society for Traumatic Stress Study
60 Revere Dr., Suite 500
Northbrook, IL 60002
(847) 480-9028

Sidran Foundation
2328 W. Joppa Rd., Suite 15
Lutherville, MD 21093
(410) 825-8888
sidran@access.digex.net (e-mail)
Provides information and advocates in support of people who have experienced trauma and have trauma-related disorders. Develops public education work-

shops on the psychological outcomes of severe childhood trauma for adult survivors, partners, caregivers, and professionals. Publishes books and educational materials on traumatic stress disorders, dissociative disorders, child sexual abuse, ritual abuse, self-injury, and self-help/recovery.

Wholistic Stress Control Institute, Inc.
P.O. Box 42481
Atlanta, GA 30311
(404) 344-2021 or (404) 755-0068
(404) 755-4333 (Fax)
Provides consultations, training, and educational resources on stress control, anger management, violence prevention, substance abuse prevention, and mental illness prevention. Develops training programs for educators, parents, children, and communities that increase coping skills and reduce the risk of high-risk behavior. Publications and training materials are available.

On-Line Information and Services

National Panic/Anxiety and Stress Disorder Newsletter
http://spiderweb.com/NPADNews

Psychology Self-Help Resources on the Net:
http://www.gasou.edu/psychweb/resource/selfhelp.htm

SUICIDE/ SURVIVORS OF SUICIDE

Suicide among the young has become the third leading cause of death. It is estimated that every 90 minutes a child or adolescent commits suicide in the U.S.
—"Children and Suicide" by W. Hahn in *Children's Needs: Psychological Perspectives,* National Association of School Psychologists, 1987.

General Information/Advocacy Groups

American Association of Suicidology
4201 Connecticut Ave NW, Suite 310
Washington, DC 20008
(202) 237-2280
(202) 237-2282 (Fax)
Sponsors conferences and training programs on suicide prevention, intervention, and working with survivors. Publications are available on suicide assessment and prediction, treatment, legal issues, special populations, crisis intervention, and directories of support programs. A publication list is available.

American Suicide Foundation
1045 Park Ave.
New York, NY 10028
(800) 531-4477
Provides state-to-state directories of survivor support groups for families and friends following a suicide.

Association of Death Education and Counseling
638 Prospect Ave.
Hartford, CT 06105
(203) 586-7503
Addresses dying, death, and bereavement issues from the professional's perspective. Membership benefits include the bimonthly newsletter *The Forum;* discounted subscriptions to journals including *Death Studies, Omega - Journal of Death and Dying, Bereavement Magazine, Thanatos, Illness, Crises and Loss,* and *The Thanatology Newsletter;* access to a wide array of printed materials on death and dying through the association's book service; and discounted registration fees to the ADEC Annual National Conference and Education Institute Programs.

International Association for Suicide Prevention
Suicide Prevention and Crisis Center
1811 Trusdale Dr.
Burlingame, GA 94010
(415) 692-6662

Hotlines/Helplines

Grief Recovery Helpline
(800) 445-4508
Provides educational services on recovering from loss.

National Youth Suicide Hotline
(800) 621-4000

Youth Crisis Hotline
(800) 448-4663
Hotline for children/adolescents who are runaways, experiencing abuse, or contemplating suicide.

Self-Help/Support Groups

Compassionate Friends
P.O. Box 3696
Oak Brook, IL 60522-3696
(708) 990-0010
Sponsors support groups across the country for parents, siblings, and friends grieving the death of a child.

On-Line Information and Services

Children and Adolescent Suicide Screening
http://indy.radiology.uiowa.edu/Providers/ClinGuide/PreventionPractice/CAScreening/05.htm

http://www.save.org/whattodo.html
Provides information on what to do if someone you know becomes suicidal.

TIC DISORDERS

A *tic* is a sudden, rapid, recurrent, nonrhythmic, stereotyped motor movement or vocalization. All forms of tic may be exacerbated by stress and attenuated during absorbing activities such as reading. **Tic Disorders** include:

Chronic Motor or Vocal Tic Disorder
Tourette's Disorder
Transient Tic Disorder

General Information/Advocacy Groups

National Institute of Neurological Disorders and Stroke
9000 Rockville Pk.
Bethesda, MD 20892
(301) 496-5751
Offers information on causes, treatment, and diagnosis of neurological disorders.

Tourette Syndrome Association
42-40 Bell Blvd.
Bayside, NY 11361
(718) 224-2999
Provides information on Tourette Syndrome, distributes publications, and two videos entitled "Tourette Syndrome: The Sudden Intruder" and "Stop it. I can't!"

Hotlines/Helplines

Tourette Syndrome Association
(800) 237-0717

Self-Help/Support Groups

Tourette Syndrome Association
42-40 Bell Blvd.
Bayside, NY 11361
(800) 237-0717
48 chapters nationwide.

On-Line Information and Services

http://neuro-www2.mgh.harvard.edu/TSA/medsci/
guidetodiagnosis.html
   Guide to the diagnosis and treatment of Tourette
   Syndrome and similar disorders.

Clearinghouses

The following organizations collect and disseminate information relating to the mental health of children and their families.

Agency for Healthcare Policy and Research
Clearinghouse
P.O. Box 8547
Silver Spring, MD 20907-8547
(800) 358-9295
Branch of the U.S. Public Health Service, goals are to promote effective, appropriate, high-quality health care, to increase access to care, and to improve the way health services are organized, delivered, and financed. The clearinghouse distributes the agency's publications, including *Clinical Treatment Guidelines for Depression in Primary Care.* A catalog is available.

American Association of Psychiatric Services for
Children
1200-C Scottsville Rd.
Rochester, NY 14624
(800) 777-6910
Conducts research and supports projects dealing with child and adolescent mental health.

Clearinghouse for Media and Technology
P.O. Box 944272
Sacramento, CA 94244
(916) 445-5103
Resource materials for people who work with students with disabilities.

Clearinghouse on Disability Information
330 C St. SW, Room 3132
Washington, DC 20202-2524
(202) 205-8241

ERIC Clearinghouse on Disabilities and Gifted
Education
Council for Exceptional Children
1920 Association Dr.
Reston, VA 20191
(800) 328-0272
(703) 620-2521 (Fax)
ericec@cec.sped.prg (e-mail)
Database of over 850,000 documents and journal articles concerning special education.

Juvenile Justice Clearinghouse
P.O. Box 6000
Rockville, MD 20850
(800) 638-8736
Provides information on child maltreatment and the response of the criminal justice system to such abuse.

National Adoption Information Clearinghouse
11426 Rockville Pike, Suite 410
Rockville, MD 20852
(301) 231-6512

National Clearinghouse for Alcohol Information
P.O. Box 2345
Rockville, MD 20852
(301) 468-2600

National Clearinghouse for Alcohol/Drug Abuse
Information
P.O. Box 2345
Rockville, MD 20847
(301) 468-2600

National Clearinghouse for the Defense of Battered
Women
125 S. 9th St., Suite 202
Philadelphia, PA 19107
(215) 351-0010
(215) 351-0779 (Fax)
Addresses battered women's self-defense issues.

National Clearinghouse on Families and Youth
P.O. Box 13505
Silver Spring, MD 20911-3505
(301) 608-8098

National Clearinghouse on Family Support and
Children's Mental Health
P.O. Box 751
Portland, OR 97207-0751
(800) 628-1696
Component of the Center for Mental Health Services' Research and Training Centers offers fact sheets on children's mental health problems, referrals to family support programs, and publications on the children's mental health service system and the empowerment of families in the system. A list of publications is available.

National Mental Health Consumer's Self-Help
Clearinghouse
  1211 Chestnut St., Suite 1000
  Philadelphia, PA 19107
  (800) 553-4539
  (215) 751-1810
  (215) 636-6310 (Fax)
  Provides consultation and technical assistance to con-
  sumer-run self-help groups nationwide and information on consumer advocacy and self-help groups
  across the country through a toll-free phone number.
  The Center also has training events and on-site consultation and distributes written materials on a variety
  of mental health topics.

National Mental Health Association Information Center
  1021 Prince St.
  Alexandria, VA 22314-5968
  (800) 969-6642
  (703) 684-5968 (Fax)
  Makes referrals to community resources and distribute
  publications of public and professional interest. A
  publications list is available.

Self-Help Clearinghouse
  Northwest Covenant Medical Center
  25 Pocono Rd.
  Denville, NJ 07834
  (201) 625-7101
  (201) 625-8848 (Fax)
  Provides information on self-help clearinghouses
  across the country and publishes a national directory
  of self-help/support groups.

Model Treatment Programs

The programs listed in this section were selected from the National Mental Health Association's Directory of Model Programs to Prevent Mental Health Disorders. *Typically, the NMHA programs are developed through research, as a collaboration between university-based investigators and community-based agencies. Other programs were selected from the psychological literature.*

Absentee Prevention Program (AAP)
  Community College of Beaver County's Prevention
  Project
  225 Center Grange Rd.
  Aliquippa, PA 15001
  (412) 775-7904
  (412) 775-7345 (Fax)
  Program goal is to prevent student absenteeism from school in an effort to promote school adjustment and achievement.

ADD Program at the Child Development Center
  University of California at Irvine
  4621 Teller, Suite 108
  Newport Beach, CA 92660
  (714) 833-8588
  Timothy Wigal, Ph.D.

Avance Family Support and Education Program
  Avance, Inc.
  301 S. Frio, Suite 310
  San Antonio, TX 78207
  (210) 270-4611
  (210) 270-4612 (Fax)
  Program goal is to improve family relations, prevent family violence, abuse and neglect, and to enhance early childhood education.

Anxiety Disorders Center
  Dept. of Psychiatry
  University of Wisconsin
  Center for Health Sciences
  600 Highland Ave.
  Madison, WI 53792
  (608) 263-6056
  Nonprofit organization provides evaluation and treatment of anxiety disorders, offers training and education for clinicians, and conducts research.

The Anxiety Treatment Center
  Nova Southeastern University
  3301 College Ave.
  Davie, FL 33314
  (305) 475-7070
  Ms. Kim Sterner, Coordinator
  Provides treatment for people ages 5 to 55 with anxiety disorders.

Biological Studies Program for Obsessive Compulsive Disorder
  Dept. of Psychiatry
  Columbia Presbyterian Medical Center
  New York, NY 10032
  (212) 960-2442

Center for the Family
  P.O. Box 157
  Corda Madera, CA 94976
  (415) 924-5750
  Cheryl VanderWaal, M.S.W., Director
  Nonprofit agency helps children of divorce and their families. Its ongoing programs include providing affordable clinical, preventative, educational and mediational services; conducting research on divorce and those factors that contribute negatively and positively to the impact on children; training mental health practitioners, clergy, attorneys, judges, pediatricians, and educators who work with disrupted families; educating the public as to the best ways to cope with divorce; and working with social policymakers on matters concerning divorce and related issues.

Center for the Treatment and Study of Anxiety
  EPPI
  Allegheny University of Health Sciences
  3200 Henry Ave.
  Philadelphia, PA 19129
  (215) 842-4010
  Dr. Edna B. Foa, Director
  Offers treatment of and research on anxiety disorders including childhood OCD.

Child and Adolescent Anxiety Disorders Clinic
Weiss Hall, 4th Floor
13th and Cecil B. Moore
Temple University
Philadelphia, PA 19122
(215) 204-7165
Provides services for children and adolescents ages 9-13 with excessive anxiety and conducts research on childhood and adolescent anxiety disorders. Treatment is free for eligible children and includes cognitive-behavioral therapy, education, and skills training in relaxation, problem-solving, self-evaluation, and modification of negative anxious thinking.

Child and Adolescent Gender Identity Clinic
Clarke Institute of Psychiatry
250 College St.
Toronto, Ontario M5T 1R8 Canada
(416) 979-4747, ext. 2271
Dr. Kenneth Zucker, Director
zucker@cs.clarke-inst.on.ca (e-mail)
Services for children who present with a suspected gender problem, or who is described as manifesting cross-sexed behavior. Children are mostly from the metropolitan Toronto area and surrounding cities, although children from other parts of Canada are seen, as well as a number of children from the U.S.

Children of Divorce Intervention Program (CODIP)
Primary Mental Health Project
575 Mt. Hope Ave.
Rochester, NY 14620
(716) 273-5957
(716) 232-6350 (Fax)
Dr. JoAnne Pedro-Carroll, Director
Program goal is to develop children's emotional adjustment and coping skills, school adjustment, and family relations.

Children's Hospital AIDS Program
Harvard AIDS Institute
Canegie Bldg., 3rd Floor
300 Longwood Ave.
Boston, MA 02115
(617) 355-6832
CHAP treats children ranging from infants to 17-year-olds with specialized care and participation in therapeutic drug trials.

Children's Outpatient Psychiatry
Children's Hospital
3665 Kearny Villa Rd., Suite 101
San Diego, CA 92123
(619) 576-5832
Provides group and individual treatment of children with OCD.

Community and Family Support Services/Healthy Start
Hawaii State Dept. of Health
2881 Waimano Home Rd., Bldg. 11
Pearl City, HI 96782
(808) 453-6020
(808) 453-6023 (Fax)
Gladys Wong, Program Coordinator
Program goal is to decrease child abuse and neglect by improving family relations, childrearing practices, parental attitudes, parent-child relations, and parent-child communication. Another goal is to work with the mother to develop such qualities as assertiveness, interpersonal interaction skills, self-esteem, social adjustment, stress management, and social skills.

Developmental Facilitation Groups for Children of Divorce
University of Michigan
Dept. of Psychiatry
3887 Taubman Center, Box 0390
University of Michigan Medical Center
Ann Arbor, MI 48109-0390
(313) 764-3167
Neil Kalter, Ph.D., Director
Program goal is to teach children to effectively cope with their parents' divorce.

Divorce and Remarriage Project
Philadelphia Child Guidance Center
Two Children's Center
34th St. and Civic Center Blvd.
Philadelphia, PA 19104
(215) 243-2600
Dr. Marion Linblad Goldberg, Director
Provides treatment, training and research.

Dougy Center for Grieving Children
3909 SE 52nd Ave.
P.O. Box 86852
Portland, OR 97286
(503) 775-5683
Non-profit support center for grieving children and families offers ongoing support groups for children and for families and many other direct and indirect services. Publishes *The Children's Grief Support Network Directory* which lists over 48 centers throughout the U.S. The cost is approximately $15 plus $4.50 shipping and handling.

Effective Parenting Information for Children (EPIC)
State University College at Buffalo
1300 Elmwood Ave.
Cassety Hall, Room 340
Buffalo, NY 14222
(716) 886-6396
(716) 886-0221 (Fax)
Marie Battaglia, Director of Development
Program goal is to provide assertiveness training, communication skills, human relations, and parenting skills through programs in drug education, self-help techniques, and a support group.

FAST (Families and Schools Together) Track, Inc.
Dept. of Psychology and Human Development
Peabody College
Vanderbilt University
Box 88, Station P.D.
Nashville, TN 37203
Kenneth A. Dodge, Ph.D., Director
(615) 322-7311
Primary and secondary intervention program focuses on working with aggressive and potentially aggressive children.

Giant Steps
c/o Giant Steps Connecticut
2475 Easton Tpke.
Fairfield, CT 06432
(203) 374-6273
Kathy Roberts, Director
Developed to meet the needs of children with neuro-integrative disorders (including autism) that impact on their ability to interact, communicate, and develop adaptive skills within their daily life. Giant Steps has

programs in Montreal, Connecticut, St. Louis, Toronto, and Australia.

Good Touch-Bad Touch
Prevention and Motivation Programs, Inc.
229 Peachtree St., NE, Suite 1212
Atlanta, GA 30303
(800) 245-1527
Pam Church, Director/Trainer
Program goal is to empower children by teaching them the skills of "body safety," which can help them prevent or stop child sexual abuse. The program teaches what abuse is and what children should do if threatened or harmed.

The Greenwich House Children's Safety Project
27 Barrow St.
New York, NY 10014
(212) 924-1091 or (212) 242-4140
Arleen Demirjian, Director
Takes a positive approach to treatment of sexually abused, battered, and neglected children by placing emphasis on empowerment rather than victimization. Classes are offered in basic safety, self-defense, and crime violence avoidance as an adjunct to individual therapy.

High/Scope Perry Preschool Project
High/Scope Educational Research Foundation
600 N. River St.
Ypsilanti, MI 48198-2898
(313) 485-2000
(313) 485-0704 (Fax)

Institute for Biobehavioral Therapy and Research
935 Northern Blvd., Suite 102
Great Neck, NY 11021
(516) 487-7116
(516) 829-1731 (Fax)
Provides individual and group psychotherapy and pharmacotherapy treating mainly OCD and any related anxiety, panic or phobia disorder, depression and schizophrenia. Institute conducts studies using experimental medications and sometimes provides free treatment for study participants. A sliding-fee scale can be arranged for eligible clients. Services are provided mainly on an in-patient basis.

Lehigh University School Psychology Program
Mountain Top Campus
111 Research Dr.
Bethlehem, PA 18015
(610) 758-6384
George DuPaul, Ph.D., Director

Lyall Preadolescent Day Treatment Program
Lyall Pavillion
Douglas Hospital
6875 Lasalle
Montreal, Quebec, Canada H4H 1R3
Dr. Natalie Grizenko, Director
Day-treatment, psychodynamically-oriented, multi-modal program treats children and families of children who are experiencing severe behavioral difficulties in the home, school, and/or community, and for whom outpatient treatment is not intensive enough. Most of the children have been diagnosed with Oppositional Defiant Disorder; 20 to 25 percent have Attention Deficit Disorder as well.

National Eating Disorders Organization
6655 S. Yale Ave.
Tulsa, OK 74136
(918) 481-4044
Laura Hill, Ph.D., Director
Provides a continuum of treatment, including outpatient, acute day treatment, and 24-hour inpatient programs.

New Beginnings Parenting Intervention (NBPI)
Arizona State University
Preventive Intervention Center
Psychology Dept., Box 871104
Tempe, AZ 85287-1104
(602) 965-7420
(602) 965-5430 (Fax)
Sharlene A. Wolchik, Professor, Psychology
Program goal is to help women of preadolescent children cope with divorce and help their children emotionally adjust by improving communication in relationships with their children.

OCD Clinic
Lucille Salter Packard Children's Hospital
Stanford University
401 Quarry Rd.
Stanford, CA 94305
(415) 497-8000
Treats children with Obsessive Compulsive Disorder who are 18 or younger.

Parents and Adolescents Can Talk (PACT)
5727 Blackwood Rd.
Bozeman, MT 59175
(406) 586-4743
Dr. Joyce B. Kohl, Project Director
Program goal is to improve parent-child communication and pro-social skills and prevent pregnancy and drug usage by training preadolescents and adolescents in assertiveness, communication skills, human relations, social skills, and drug, sex and health education.

Parents as Teachers (PAT)
Parents as Teachers National Center, Inc.
10176 Corporate Square Dr., Suite 230
St. Louis, MO 63132
(314) 432-4330
(314) 432-8963 (Fax)
Mildred Winter, Executive Director
Program goal is to prevent academic failure by promoting positive parent-school relationships and child-rearing practices within the family.

Pediatric Enuresis Clinic
Children's Hospital at Stanford
Dept. of Urology, Room S287
Stanford, CA 94305-5118
(415) 725-5530
Lisa Harris, Director
Specializes in the care and treatment of children who have persistent nighttime and/or daytime wetting.

Pre-School Stress Relief Program
Wholistic Stress Control Institute
2545 Benjamin E Mays SW
Atlanta, GA 30311
(404) 344-2021
(404) 755-4333 (Fax)
Gloria S. Elder, Project Director
Substance abuse and mental health program for day care and school teachers to use with children teaches coping skills for reducing and managing stress for students in high risk environments. There is also a stress reduction workshop for families. A six-week curriculum covers positive self-image, awareness of feelings, understanding of body changes, stress coping skills, and appropriate releases of anger. Materials are available for teachers to implement the program in their school and/or community.

Primary Mental Health Project (PMHP)
Reach Out to Schools: School Competency Program
Stone Center
Wellesley College
Wellesley, MA 02181
(617) 283-3778
(617) 283-3646 (Fax)
Pamela Seigle, Project Director
Program goal is to improve teacher-student interactions and prevent violence by providing training in communication skills, human relations, social skills, and parenting.

Primary Mental Health Project
University of Rochester Center for Community Study
575 Mt. Hope Ave.
Rochester, NY 14620
(716) 273-5957
(716) 232-6350 (Fax)
Dr. A. Dirk Hightower, Director
School-based program prevents or detects early young children's school adjustment problems.

Project TEACCH (Treatment and Education of Autistic and Related Communication Handicapped Children and Adults)
University of North Carolina
310 Medical School Wing E, C.B. 7180
Chapel Hill, NC 27599
(919) 966-2174
North Carolina's agency for the identification and treatment of autism provides comprehensive teacher training for working with autistic children, classrooms in the public schools, support for families in their efforts to keep their children at home, and educational assessment and curriculum materials that are integrated with its overall approach.

PUSH for Youths GOALS
Institute for Study of Children, Families and the Community
Eastern Michigan University
102 King Hall
Ypsilanti, MI 48197
(313) 487-0374
Curriculum assists foster parents as primary teachers of youths approaching emancipation from foster care and is divided into four modules: Self-Help Skills, Choices and Consequences, Employability, and Leaving Home Again.

Rainbows
1111 Tower Rd.
Schaumburg, IL 60173
(847) 310-1880
(847) 310-0120 (Fax)
Offers 12-week support program for youth coping with a significant loss either through death or divorce.

Resource Center on Child Protection and Custody in Domestic Violence Situations
P.O. Box 8970
Reno, NV 89507
(800) 527-3223
Provides information, materials, consultation, technical assistance, and legal research related to child protection and custody within the context of domestic violence. A publications list is available.

Rosemont Center
  2440 Dawnlight Ave.
  Columbus, OH 43211
  (614) 471-2626
  Treatment facility for children and adolescents offers residential treatment, day treatment, substance abuse programs, group homes, family services, and other services for the child and family.

School Development Program (SDP)
  Yale Child Study Center
  P.O. Box 207900
  230 South Frontage Rd.
  New Haven, CT 06520-7900
  (203) 785-2548
  (203) 785-3359 (Fax)
  James P. Comer, M.D., Director
  Program goal is to enhance academic achievement in the school and to improve the parent-school relationship.

Sciacca Comprehensive Service Development for Mental Illness, Drug Addiction, and Substance Abuse
  299 Riverside Dr.
  New York, NY 10025
  (212) 866-5935

Specialized Alternatives for Families and Youth of America (SAFY)
  10100 Elida Rd.
  Delphos, OH 45833
  (800) 532-7239
  SAFY manages therapeutic foster care programs in Ohio, Indiana, South Carolina, Oklahoma, Nevada, and Texas. The programs include treatment foster care, respite foster care, transitional foster care, medically fragile foster care, aftercare programs, in-home interventions, independent/shared living programs, and sex offender services in foster care setting.

Steps Toward Effective, Enjoyable Parenting (STEEP)
  University of Minnesota
  12 McNeal Hall
  1985 Buford
  St. Paul, MN 55108
  (612) 626-1212
  (612) 626-1210 (Fax)
  Martha Farrell Erickson, Ph.D., Coordinator

Program goal is to promote healthy parent-infant interaction and prevent family violence.

Students Together and Resourceful (STAR)
  Georgia State University
  Dept. of Psychology
  University Plaza
  Atlanta, GA 30303-3083
  (404) 651-2029
  James G. Emshoff, Ph.D., Director
  Program goal is to prevent children of substance-abusing parents from suffering from a variety of psychosocial problems (addiction, antisocial behavior, poor school performance, poor relationship skills, and depression) for which they are at increased risk.

Super II
  Metropolitan Atlanta Council on Alcohol and Drugs, Inc.
  2045 Peachtree Rd. NE, Suite 605
  Atlanta, GA 30309
  (404) 351-1800
  (404) 351-2840 (Fax)
  Gregg Raduka, Ph.D., NCAC II, Projects Director
  Program goal is to prevent initial drug usage by creating healthy parent-child communication and improved self-esteem.

Super Stars
  2045 Peachtree Rd. NE, Suite 605
  Atlanta, GA 30309
  (404) 351-1800
  (404) 351-2840 (Fax)
  Greg Raduka
  Program goal is to reduce drug usage by strengthening self-esteem through parent-child communication.

Systematic Training for Effective Parenting (STEP)
  American Guidance Service
  4201 Woodland Rd.
  Circle Pines, MN 55014
  (612) 786-4343
  Program goal is to strengthen family relationships by teaching effective childrearing techniques, parent-child communication, family relations, and by building the children's self-esteem.

Tri-State Sleep Disorders Center
  Enuresis Division
  1275 E. Kemper Rd.
  Cincinnati, OH 45246
  (513) 671-3101
  Martin Scharf, Ph.D., Director
  Treatment program for enuretic children emphasizes a comprehensive, multimodal approach combining bladder-stretching exercises, stream interruption, counseling for motivation and responsibility, visual sequencing, and conditioning therapy.

American Association of Psychiatric Services for Children
    1200-C Scottsville Rd.
    Rochester, NY 14624
    (800) 777-6910
    Acts as information clearinghouse; conducts research and supports projects dealing with child and adolescent mental health.

Association for the Care of Children's Health
    7910 Woodmont Ave., Suite 300
    Bethesda, MD 20814
    (301) 654-6549

Center for Evaluation of Child Mental Health Systems
    Judge Baker Children's Center
    295 Longwood Ave.
    Boston, MA 02115
    (617) 232-8390
    (617) 232-4125 (Fax)
    Provides consultation and training on the evaluation of children's mental health systems and on-site consultation on management information systems to state mental health agencies.

Children's Emotions Anonymous
    P.O. Box 4245
    St. Paul, MN 55104
    (612) 647-9712
    Offers 12-step program to improve the emotional health of children aged 5-12.

Council for Children with Behavioral Disorders
    1920 Association Dr.
    Reston, VA 22091
    (703) 620-3660
    Works to improve educational programs for children with emotional and behavioral disturbances.

EMDR International Association (Eye Movement Desensitization and Reprocessing)
    P.O Box 51010
    Pacific Grove, CA 93950-6010
    (408) 372-3900
    (408) 647-9881 (Fax)
    inst@emdr.com (e-mail)
    Provides professional and educational support to clinicians and researchers interested in the clinical intervention EMDR; develops practice guidelines and standards for the use of EMDR and distribute publications; sponsors training institutes across the country.

Father Flanagan's Boys' Home (Boys Town)
    Boys Town, NE 68010
    (402) 498-3200
    (402) 498-1125 (Fax)
    (800) 448-3000 (National Hotline)
    Publishes low-cost and free materials on issues related to youth such as school problems, learning disabilities, eating disorders, abuse, divorce etc.

Fathers' Network
    P.O. Box 800-SH
    San Anselmo, CA 94979-0800
    (415) 453-2839
    Aims to increase involvement of fathers in parenting, to encourage mutually fulfilling relationships between fathers and their children, and to challenge traditional "provider" role regardless of marital/custodial status.

Federation for Children with Special Needs
    95 Berkeley St., Suite 104
    Boston, MA 02173
    (617) 482-2915 or (800) 331-0688
    (617) 695-2935 (Fax)
    Coalition of parent groups offers a variety of services to parents of children with varying disabilities.

Federation of Families for Children's Mental Health
    1021 Prince St.
    Alexandria, VA 22314
    (703) 684-7710
    (703) 836-1040 (Fax)

Global Nomads International
    P.O. Box 9584
    Washington, DC 20016-9584
    (703) 993-2975 or (703) 758-7766
    (703) 993-2966 or (703) 758-7766 (Fax)
    info@gni.org (e-mail)
    Provides support to children of all ages and nationalities who have lived abroad or relocated with their families a great deal.

Information Exchange on Young Adult Chronic Patients
20 Squadron Blvd., Suite 400
New City, NY 10956
(914) 634-0050
Gathers and disseminates information about treatment programs/methods for persons who have needed mental health services for at least two years.

Institute for Mental Health Initiatives
4545 42nd St. NW, Suite 311
Washington, DC 20016
(202) 364-7111
(202) 363-3891 (Fax)
Promotes mental health through public information and helps television, film, radio, and print media professionals gain insight into human emotions and portray conflict and violence responsibly.

Institute for Research in Hypnosis and Psychotherapy
5 West 73rd St.
New York, NY 10023
(212) 874-5290

Intensive Family Preservation Services
Edna McConnell Clark Foundation
250 Park Ave., Suite 900
New York, NY 10177-0026
(212) 551-9100
Makes available a listing of agencies throughout the U.S. that provide Intensive Family Preservation Services.

Matrix Research Institute
6008 Wayne Ave.
Philadelphia, PA 19144
(215) 438-8200
(215) 438-8337 (Fax)
WORKMRI@aol.com (e-mail)
Research and training center provides program evaluation and systems analysis, professional training and human resource development, and public education and consultation services across the mental health, mental retardation, aging, substance abuse, and physical disability fields. Publications are available on such topics as psychosocial rehabilitation, employment programming, consumer and family empowerment, and Social Security Benefit programs.

Mental Health Policy Resource Center
1730 Rhode Island Ave., Suite 308
Washington, DC 20036
(202) 775-8826
(202) 659-7613 (Fax)

NAMI Child and Adolescent Network
200 N. Glebe Rd., Suite 1015
Arlington, VA 22203-3754
(703) 524-7600
Advocacy organization provides support to people with mental illnesses and their families and friends. NAMI chapters with child and adolescent networks provide information, education, and support to families of children with emotional and behavioral disturbances.

National Alliance for the Mentally Ill
2101 Wilson Blvd., Suite 200
Arlington, VA 22201
(800) 950-6264
Fosters local self-help groups and offers information/referral, guidance and support for families, advocacy services, and resource materials.

National Association for Self-Esteem
P.O. Box 277877
Sacramento, CA 95827
(800) 488-6273
Brings personal worth, responsibility, and integrity to individuals, families, schools, government, and the workplace.

National Center for Education in Maternal and Child Health
2000 15th St. North, Suite 701
Arlington, VA 22201-2617
(703) 524-7802
(703) 524-9335 (Fax)

National Center for Health Statistics
6525 Belcrest Rd., Room 1064
Data Dissemination Branch
Hyattsville, MD 20782
(301) 436-8500
Information on health that includes statistics on suicide, serious mental illness and disability in the U.S., and office visits to psychiatrists.

National Coalition of Hispanic Health and Human
Service Organizations
  1501 16th St. NW
  Washington, DC 20036-1401
  (202) 387-5000
  (202) 797-4353 (Fax)

National Health Information Center
  P.O. Box 1133
  Washington, DC 20013-1133
  (800) 336-4797
  (301) 984-4256 (Fax)
  Helps the public and professionals locate health information through identification of health information resources, an information and referral system, and publications. Directories on health information resources and a publication list are available.

National Information and Resource Service
  P.O. Box 4008
  Austin, TX 78765
  (800) 531-5305
  Maintains a database of specialized psychiatric and rehabilitative services nationwide.

National Institute of Mental Health (NIMH)
  Public Information Branch
  5600 Fishers Lane, Room 7C-02
  Rockville, MD 20857
  (301) 443-4513
  Conducts research on the causes, treatment, and prevention of mental disorders. The Public Information Branch provides information on the NIMH and distributes free publications on various mental disorders for the general public and research and scientific materials for professionals. A publications catalog is available.

National Mental Health Association
  1021 Prince St.
  Alexandria, VA 22314
  (800) 969-6642
  A grassroots advocacy movement dedicated to addressing all aspects of America's mental health and mental illness. Local and state chapters work to improve services, prevent mental illness, and promote mental health. Publishes *The NMHA Directory of Model Programs to Prevent Mental Disorders and Promote*

Mental Health and *The NMHA Guide to Establishing Community-Based Prevention Programs.*

National Prevention Coalition
  1021 Prince St.
  Alexandria, VA 22314
  (703) 684-7722
  Advocates on behalf of prevention and mental health promotion. Over 25 national mental health organizations comprise its membership.

National Research and Training Center on Psychiatric
Disabilities and Peer Support
  University of Illinois at Chicago
  104 S. Michigan Ave., Suite 900
  Chicago, IL 60603
  (312) 422-8180
  Disseminates information, conducts research, and provides training and technical assistance to health care professionals working with people with psychiatric disabilities. It offers innovative approaches that enhance service delivery for this population. Publications are available on topics related to the full spectrum of psychosocial rehabilitation, with an emphasis on vocational and employment issues.

National Resource Center for Crisis Nurseries and
Respite Care Services
  Chapel Hill Training-Outreach Project
  800 Eastowne Dr., Suite 105
  Chapel Hill, NC 27514
  (800) 473-1727
  Provides support and technical assistance to crisis nursery and respite care service providers. Fact sheets and general resource sheets, including state contact sheets, are available about respite care and crisis nurseries.

National Resource Institute on Children with Handicaps
  University of Washington
  CDMRC WJ-10
  Seattle, WA 98195
  (206) 543-2213
  Provides resources to practitioners working with children with disabilities and their families.

National Resource Network on Child and Family Mental Health Services
Washington Business Group on Health
777 N. Capitol St. NE, Suite 800
Washington, DC 20002
(202) 408-9320
(202) 408-9332 (Fax)
Provides assistance in developing family focused, culturally competent, community-based, multi-agency service delivery systems to 22 Child and Family Mental Health Services grantee sites who serve children with serious emotional disturbance and their families; sponsors teleconferences and seminars and conducts one-on-one consultations to the 22 grantees.

National Technical Assistance Center for Children's Mental Health
3307 M St. NW
Georgetown University Child Development Center
Washington, DC 20007-3935
(202) 687-5000
(202) 687-5034 (Fax)

Physicians for Human Rights
100 Boylston St., Suite 702
Boston, MA 02116
(617) 695-0041
(617) 695-0307 (Fax)

PsychScapes
Mental Health Workshops and Conferences Registry
University Park
P.O. Box 101480
Denver, CO 80250-1480
(303) 333-9034
(303) 733-1541 (Fax)
Offers a listing of mental health related conferences and workshops nationwide that is available by subscription.

Recovery, Inc. International Headquarters
802 N. Dearborn St.
Chicago, IL 60610
(312) 337-5661
(312) 337-5756 (Fax)
International network of mutual aid support groups for people with mental illness and their families fosters weekly group meetings that follow the Recovery method of self-help techniques that help prevent relapse. Publications on the Recovery method are available.

Research and Training Center on Family Support and Children's Mental Health
Portland State University
P.O. Box 751
Portland, OR 97207-0751
(503) 725-4040
(503) 725-4180 (Fax)
Conducts research on the child mental health service system and provides training and technical assistance to individuals and organizations working on behalf of children with emotional and/or behavioral disorders. The Center's activities are based on the tenets of the Comprehensive Service System model that stresses the importance of community based, family centered, and culturally appropriate services for children and their families.

Sibling Information Network
1776 Ellington Rd.
South Windsor, CT 06074
(203) 648-1205
Makes available information, support, projects, and literature for families with members who have emotional or behavioral disabilities.

Sibling Support Project
Children's Hospital and Medical Center
P.O. Box 5371, CL-09
Seattle, WA 98105
(206) 368-4912

Society for Education and Research in Psychiatric Nursing
437 Twin Bay Dr.
Pensacola, FL 32534-1350
(904) 474-9024
(904) 484-8762 (Fax)

World Institute on Disability
510 16th St.
Oakland, CA 94612
(510) 763-4100
(510) 763-4109 (Fax)

Young Adult Institute and Workshop
460 W. 34th St., 11th Floor
New York, NY 10001
(212) 563-7474
Programs enable persons with mental retardation,
learning disabilities, or emotional illness to progress
toward a more "normal" life.

Youth Emotions Anonymous
P.O. Box 4245
St. Paul, MN 55104
(612) 647-9712
Offers 12-step program designed to improve the
emotional health of adolescents and teens ages 13-18.

American Academy of Child and Adolescent Psychiatry
3615 Wisconsin Ave. NW
Washington, DC 20016
(800) 333-7636
(202) 966-2891 (Fax)
Membership organization with over 6,000 child and adolescent psychiatrists offers information and publications relating to adolescent and child psychiatry for parents and professionals. The academy also makes referrals to child and adolescent psychiatrists nationwide.

American Association for Marriage and Family Therapy
1133 15th St. NW, Suite 300
Washington, DC 20005
(202) 452-0109
(202) 223-2329 (Fax)
Professional association that gives accreditation/licensing to mental health professionals in the field of marriage and family therapy, promotes the practice of marriage and family therapy through research, theory development, education, and the "credentialing" of professionals. The association provides individuals with the tools and resources they need to succeed as marriage and family therapists. It hosts conferences and training workshops and publishes journals, professional materials, and general information pamphlets.

American Association for Partial Hospitalization
301 North Fairfax St., Suite 109
Alexandria, VA 22314
(703) 836-2274
(703) 836-0083 (Fax)
Professional trade association helps people who are in partial hospitalization and ambulatory care.

American Association of Children's Residential Centers
1021 Prince St.
Alexandria, VA 22314-2971
(703) 838-7522
(703) 684-5968 (Fax)
Represents residential care facilities for children; provides trainings, seminars, and conferences for member organizations; and publishes a journal.

American Association of Community Psychiatrists
P.O. Box 1990
Clackamas, OR 97015

American Dance Therapy Association
1000 Century Plaza Suite 230
Columbia, MD 21044
(410) 997-4040

American Family Therapy Academy
2020 Pennsylvania Ave. NW, Suite 273
Washington, DC 20006
(202) 994-2776
(202) 994-2775 (Fax)
Membership association for family therapists.

The American Group Psychotherapy Association
25 E. 21st St., 6th Floor
New York, NY 10010
(212) 477-2677
Provides its members with professional development and continuing education opportunities in all aspects of group psychotherapy to enhance clinical skills and career advancement, including educational programs, publications, research and teaching, networking and practice development, as well as membership in local and regional affiliate societies.

American Mental Health Counselors Association
801 N. Fairfax St., Suite 304
Alexandria, VA 22304
(800) 326-2642
(703) 548-4775 (Fax)
Nonprofit membership association.

American Orthopsychiatric Association
330 7th Ave., 18th Floor
New York, NY 10001
(212) 564-5930
(212) 564-6180 (Fax)

American Psychiatric Association
1400 K St. NW
Washington, DC 20005
(202) 682-6000
(202) 682-6114 (Fax)

American Psychological Association
750 First St. NE
Washington, DC 20002
(202) 336-5500

American Psychological Society
1010 Vermont Ave. NW, Suite 1100
Washington, DC 20005-1907
(202) 783-2077
(202) 783-2083 (Fax)

Association of Black Psychologists
P.O. Box 55999
Washington, DC 20040
(202) 722-0808

Association of Child and Adolescent Psychiatric Nurses
1211 Locust St.
Philadelphia, PA 19107
(800) 826-2950

Association of Mental Health Administrators
60 Revere Dr., Suite 500
Northbrook, IL 60062
(847) 480-9626
(847) 480-9282 (Fax)

Black Psychiatrists of America
P.O. Box 1758
North Little Rock, AR 72115

Consortium for Social Science Associations
1522 K St. NW, Suite 836
Washington, DC 20005
(202) 842-3525
(202) 842-2788 (Fax)

International Association of Eating Disorders Professionals
123 NW 13th St., #766
Boca Raton, FL 33432
(800) 800-8126

International Association of Psychosocial Rehabilitation Services
10025 Governor Warfield Pkwy.
Columbia, MD 21044
(410) 730-7190
(410) 730-5965 (Fax)

National Association for Music Therapy
8455 Colesville Rd., Suite 930
Silver Spring, MD 20901
(301) 589-3300

National Association for Poetry Therapy
P.O. Box 551
Port Washington, NY 11050
(516) 944-9791

National Association of School Psychologists
8455 Colesville Rd., Suite 1000
Silver Spring, MD 20910
(301) 657-0270

National Association of Social Workers
750 First St. NE, Suite 700
Washington, DC 20002-4241
(800) 638-8799
(202) 336-8310 (Fax)
Largest professional organization of social workers. Major activities include maintaining professional standards; offering credentials; publishing books, journals, and reference works; shaping public policy to assist the disadvantaged and disenfranchised; providing technical assistance; and advancing the profession through provision of continuing education and conferences.

National Federation of Societies for Clinical Social Work
P.O. Box 3740
Arlington, VA 22203
(703) 552-3866
(703) 522-9441 (Fax)

Organizations for Mental Health Issues Affecting Minorities

AFRICAN AMERICAN

Association of Black Psychologists
P.O. Box 55999
Washington, DC 20040
(202) 722-0808

Black Psychiatrists of America
P.O. Box 1758
North Little Rock, AR 72115

National Association of Black Social Workers
8436 W. McNichols
Detroit, MI 48221
(313) 862-6700

National Black Child Development Institute
1023 15th St. NW, Suite 600
Washington, DC 20002
(202) 387-1281

National Black Women's Health Project
1237 Ralph David Abernathy Blvd. SW
Atlanta, GA 30310
(404) 758-9590

ASIAN/ASIAN AMERICAN

National Asian Pacific American Families Against Substance Abuse, Inc.
1887 Maplegate St.
Monterey Park, CA 91755
(213) 278-0031
(213) 278-9078 (Fax)

National Research Center on Asian-American Mental Health
UCLA
405 Hilgard Ave.
Los Angeles, CA 90024-1563
(310) 825-1775

Southeast Asia Action Resource Center
1628 16th St. NW, 3rd Floor
Washington, DC 20009
(202) 667-4690
(202) 667-6449 (Fax)

LATINO/HISPANIC

Boys Town National Hotline
13940 Gutowski Rd.
Boys Town, NE 68010
(800) 448-3000
(402) 498-1875 (Fax)
Crisis line and information referral hotline for families and children/adolescents who are runaways, experiencing abuse, or contemplating suicide. Also provides Spanish speaking teleprompter. 24-hour service both in English and Spanish.

Casa La Esperanza
1241 Lafayette Ave.
Bronx, NY 10474
(718) 918-1935
Social community run by and for persons suffering mental illness provides a transitional job program and job training service and produces newsletter on what's happening in the program. Members are responsible for planning their social events, meals, and meal service.

National Coalition of Hispanic Health and Human Service Organizations
1501 16th St., NW
Washington, DC 20036-1401
(202) 387-5000
(202) 797-4353 (Fax)

Spanish Language Mental Health Hotline
(202) 291-4740

NATIVE AMERICAN

American Indian Health Care Association
245 East 6th St., Suite 499
St. Paul, MN 55101
(800) 473-1926

Indian Mental Health Program
5300 Homestead Rd. NE
Albuquerque, NM 87110
(505) 837-4245

Native American Women's Health Education Resource
Center
  P.O. Box 572
  Lake Andes, SD 57356
  (605) 487-7072

National Association for Native American Children of
Alcoholics
  1402 Third Ave., Suite 1110
  Seattle, WA 98101
  (800) 322-5601
  (206) 467-7686 (Fax)

U.S. Indian Health Service
  5600 Fishers Lane
  Parklawn Bldg., Room 6-35
  Rockville, MD 20857
  (301) 443-3593

GENERAL

Minority Research Training Program
  American Psychiatric Association
  1400 K St. NW
  Washington, DC 20005
  (800) 852-1390
  Program is designed to increase the number of minorities entering the field of psychiatric research. The program provides medical students and psychiatric residents with funding for stipends, travel expenses, and related training costs for an elective or summer experience in a research environment, with specific attention paid to their career development in research. Stipends are also available for postresidency fellowships for minority psychiatrists.

REGIONAL RESOURCES

Center for Support of Mental Health Services in Isolated Rural Areas
University of Denver
Denver, CO 80208
(303) 871-3099
Offers training and assistance to rural organizations providing mental health services. Provides assistance with human resource development and sponsor conferences, workshops, demonstrations, and evaluations.

Farm Resource Center
P.O. Box 87
Mound City, IL 62963
(800) 851-4719
Nonprofit organization provides mental health and human services to citizens living in rural farming and/or coal mining communities in Illinois and West Virginia. The center provides outreach and counseling services.

Mid-Atlantic Network of Youth and Family Services
9400 McKnight Rd., #204
Pittsburgh, PA 15237
(412) 366-6562
(412) 366-5407 (Fax)
Regional organization of service providers designed to strengthen and coordinate resources and services for youth and families in high-risk situations. The network provides training and technical assistance, resources, and coordination for its member agencies and other groups involved in services to youth and families. The network publishes a directory of organizations serving youths and families in the Mid-Atlantic region (Delaware, Maryland, Pennsylvania, Virginia, West Virginia, and the District of Columbia).

National Association for Rural Mental Health
337 East Ferguson Ave., Box 570
Wood River, IL 62095
(618) 251-0589
(618) 251-6246 (Fax)

National Rural Health Association
One West Armour Blvd., Suite 301
Kansas City, MO 64111
(816) 756-3140

Works to improve the health of rural Americans through advocacy, education, and research. It provides consultation to rural health care workers and helps build multidisciplined networks of rural health care professionals working on the grass-roots level across the country. The association publishes newsletters, journals, and publications and sponsors workshops and continuing education activities.

New England Organization of Child and Adolescent Psychiatry
124 Mt. Auburn St.
Cambridge, MA 02138
(617) 354-4060

Western Interstate Commission for Higher Education
Mental Health Program
P.O. Box 9752
Boulder, CO 80301-9752
(303) 541-0250
(303) 541-0291 (Fax)
WICHE is a regional agency comprised of 15 western states. The Mental Health Program exchanges resources, expertise, and information with educators, mental health practitioners, and administrators to improve the quality of training and research in the mental health field. Publications are available on such topics as diversity in the mental health service system, managed care, workforce training, and service system research.

STATE RESOURCES

ALABAMA

Alabama Alliance for the Mentally Ill
6900 Sixth Ave. South, Suite B
Birmingham, AL 35212-1902
(205) 833-8336
(205) 833-8309 (Fax)

Alabama Curriculum Assistance
State Department of Education
207 Montgomery St.
Bell Building, #815
Montgomery, AL 36104
(334) 242-8059

Mental Health Association of Alabama
6020 Camelot Ct.
Montgomery, AL 36104
(334) 262-5500
Provides parental support program through mental health associations in Montgomery.

Mental Health Consumers of Alabama
P.O. Box 70459
Montgomery, AL 36107-0459
(800) 264-6422
(334) 834-6398 (Fax)

ALASKA

Alaska Alliance for the Mentally Ill
110 West 15th Ave., Suite B
Anchorage, AK 99501
(907) 277-1300
(907) 277-1400 (Fax)

Mental Health Consumers of Alaska
430 West 7th Ave., #220
Anchorage, AK 99501
(907) 277-3817
(907) 277-2193 (Fax)

ARIZONA

Arizona Alliance for the Mentally Ill
2441 East Fillmore St.
Phoenix, AZ 85008-6033
(602) 244-8166
(602) 220-0934 (Fax)

Arizona Center for Disability Law
3839 North 3rd St., Suite 209
Phoenix, AZ 85012
(800) 927-2260
(602) 274-6779 (Fax)

Arizona Organization of Child and Adolescent Psychiatry
430 N. Tucson Blvd.
Tucson, AZ 85716
(602) 325-4837

ARKANSAS

Arkansas Alliance for the Mentally Ill
Hendrix Hall, Room 233
4313 W Markham St.
Little Rock, AR 72205-4096
(501) 661-1548
(501) 664-0264 (Fax)

Arkansas Federation of Families for Children's Mental Health
4313 W. Markham St.
Little Rock, AR 72205-4096
(501) 686-9060

Child, Adolescent and Family Guidance Center
11825 Hinson, Suite 101
Little Rock, AR 72212
(501) 228-7500

P.E.O.P.L.
4313 W. Markham St.
Hendricks Hall, Suite 160
Little Rock, AR 72205-4096
(800) 237-3675
(501) 686-9273 (Fax)
P.E.O.P.L (Personal Empowerment of the Psychiatrically Labeled) offers statewide treatment, counseling, and personal enhancement therapy for people with mental illness. Also serves as an advocacy group.

CALIFORNIA

Alameda County Parental Stress Service
1727 Martin Luther King, #109
Oakland, CA 94612
(800) 829-3777

California Alliance for the Mentally Ill
1111 Howe Ave., Suite 475
Sacramento, CA 95825-8541
(916) 567-0163
(916) 567-1757 (Fax)

California InterNetwork of Mental Health Clients
Computer Mailing List
   Family Network of California
   389 Bryce Canyon Rd.
   San Rafael, CA 94903
   (415) 479-3531
   (415) 479-3531 (Fax)
   listproc@thecity.sfsu.edu (e-mail)
   SylviaC@netcom.com (Internet)
   Operates the electronic mailing list for the California
   Network of Mental Health Clients. The focus of the
   list is to discuss California legislation, implementation
   of legislation in the counties, and issues with local
   mental health boards, self-help organizations, managed care and other related topics. To subscribe to the
   list send an e-mail message to:
   m mail listserv@thecity.sfsu.edu
   The command in the body of the message should read:
   subscribe cinmhc your firstname your lastname.

Parental Stress Hotline/Teenline
   Family Service - Mid-Peninsula
   Palo Alto, CA 94306
   (415) 327-3333
   Offers support to parents struggling with family, parenting, personal, and job-related stress who reside in
   Santa Clara and San Mateo counties. The Teenline
   helps teenagers who are having problems with family
   or peer relationships, school, life decisions, abuse, and
   other emotional issues. Services include emotional
   support, information, and referrals.

United Advocates for Children of California
   965 Mission St., Suite 405
   San Francisco, CA 94103
   (415) 882-6249

COLORADO

Colorado Alliance for the Mentally Ill
   1100 Filmore St.
   Denver, CO 80206-3334
   (303) 321-3104
   (303) 321-0912 (Fax)

Colorado Federation of Families for Children's Mental
Health
   6795 E. Tennessee Ave., 425
   Denver, CO 80204
   (303) 377-3040
   (303) 377-4920 (Fax)

Colorado Organization of Child and Adolescent
Psychiatry
   1735 Alkire
   Golden, CO 80401
   (303) 979-6310

Denver Coalition of Mental Health Consumers and
Groups
   8851 East Florida #112
   Denver, CO 80231
   (303) 377-8406

4 Parents Helpline
   1391 North Speer Blvd., Suite 400
   Denver, CO 80204
   (800) 288-3444
   (303) 534-2543 (Fax)
   Parent advocate organization offers a confidential non-
   medical "warm line" providing support information
   and referrals to parents and those working with children throughout Colorado.

North Colorado Federation of Families for Children's
Mental Health
   1400 Whitepeak Ct.
   Ft. Collins, CO 80525
   (970) 223-3036

Vietnamese Mental Health Support Group
   1818 Gaylord St.
   Denver, CO 80206

You Are Not Alone
   1620 Mathews #303
   Fort Collins, CO 80524

CONNECTICUT

Connecticut Alliance for the Mentally Ill
  151 New Park Ave.
  Hartford, CT 06106
  (203) 586-2319
  (203) 586-7477 (Fax)

Connecticut Association for Children with Learning Disabilities
  18 Marshall St.
  South Norwalk, CT 06854
  (203) 838-5010
  Offers informational materials, referrals, and consultations. An "Info Line" is established to answer questions from parents and professionals. The CACLID resource center has a reference and research library as well as a bookstore for those interested in the most up-to-date information about learning disabilities.

Connecticut Clearinghouse
  334 Farmington Ave.
  Plainville, CT 06062
  (800) 232-4424
  Provides information about self-help/support groups in Connecticut.

Connecticut Federation of Families for Children's Mental Health
  20-30 Beaver Rd.
  Wethersfield, CT 06109
  (203) 529-6552
  (203) 529-6833 (Fax)
  Parent advocacy group.

Connecticut Self-Help Mutual Support Network
  389 Whitney Ave.
  New Haven, CT 06511
  (203) 789-7645

DISTRICT OF COLUMBIA

Alliance for the Mentally Ill - DC Threshold
  422 8th St. SE
  Washington, DC 20003-2832
  (202) 546-0646
  (202) 546-6817 (Fax)

Mental Health Association of DC
  1628 16th St NW
  Washington, DC 20010
  (202) 265-6363
  (202) 265-8357 (Advocacy Dept.)

Family Advocacy and Support Association Inc.
  P.O. Box 74884
  Washington, DC 20056-4884
  (202) 576-6065 or (202) 576-7157

Greater Washington DC Self-Help Clearinghouse
  Mental Health Association of Northern Virginia
  7630 Little River Tpke., Suite 206
  Annandale, VA 22003
  (703) 941-5465
  Provides information on self-help/support groups for the Washington, DC, Metropolitan area.

DELAWARE

Alliance for the Mentally Ill of Delaware
  2500 W. 4th St. Plaza, Suite 12
  Wilmington, DE 19805
  (888) 427-2643
  (302) 427-2075 (Fax)
  Provides support/outreach services, psychiatric referrals, information on mental health services available in Delaware, and advocacy.

Delaware Mental Health Consumer Coalition
  278 E. Chestnuthill Rd.
  Newark, DE 19713
  (302) 455-9456

Delaware Organization of Child and Adolescent Psychiatry
  Alfred I. duPont Institute
  1600 Rockland
  P.O. Box 269
  Wilmington, DE 19899-0269
  (302) 651-4500

Mental Health Association of Delaware
1813 North Franklin St.
Wilmington, DE 19802
(302) 656-8308
(302) 656-0747 (Fax)

FLORIDA

Florida Family Organization for Individuals with Brain Disorders
304 N. Meridian St., Suite 2
Tallahassee, FL 32301
(904) 222-3400
(904) 222-5675 (Fax)

Lee Davis Neighborhood Development Center
2705 E. Dr.
MLK Jr. Blvd.
Tampa, FL 33610
(813) 989-1890
(813) 248-4535 (Fax)
Parent advocacy group.

United Families for Children's Mental Health
5510 Gray St., Suite 220
Tampa, FL 33609
(813) 523-1130
Parent advocacy group.

GEORGIA

Georgia Alliance for the Mentally Ill
1256 Briarcliff Rd. NE, Room 412-S
Atlanta, GA
(404) 894-8860
(404) 894-8862 (Fax)

Georgia Mental Health Consumer Network
246 Sycamore St., Suite 100
Decatur, GA 30030
(800) 297-6146

Georgia Parent Support Network
620 Peachtree St. NE, #300E
Atlanta, GA 30308
(404) 875-6801

HAWAII

Hawaii Families as Allies
200 N. Vineyard Blvd., Suite 300
Honolulu, HI 96817
(808) 521-1846
(808) 533-6995 (Fax)
Parent advocacy group.

Hawaii State Alliance for the Mentally Ill
1126 12th Ave., Suite 205
Honolulu, HI 96816-3714
(808) 737-2778
(808) 734-3477 (Fax)

United Self-Help
277 Ohua Ave.
Honolulu, HI 96815
(808) 926-0466

IDAHO

Boise Alliance for the Mentally Ill
313 North Allumbaugh
Boise, ID 83704
(208) 376-4304

Family Organization for People with Brain Disorders
331 N. Allumbaugh St.
Boise, ID 83704-9208
(208) 376-2143

Community, Loving, Understanding, Belonging (CLUB)
150 Shoup Ave., Suite 19
Idaho Falls, ID 83402

Idaho Parents Unlimited
4696 Overland Rd., #478
Boise, ID 83705
(208) 342-5884
(208) 342-1408 (Fax)

ILLINOIS

BNICEH (Black Network in Children's Emotional
Health)
6951 North Sheridan Rd.
Chicago, IL 60626-3527
(312) 973-7124
(312) 666-2316 (Fax)
Parent advocacy group.

Equip for Equality Inc.
11 East Adams, Suite 1200
Chicago, IL 60603
(312) 341-0022
(312) 341-0295 (Fax)
State protection and advocacy agency.

Illinois Tele-Help
P.O. Box 128
Glencoe, IL 60022
(874) 291-0085
Provides information about mental health
self-help/support groups for Illinois.

Illinois Federation of Families
15 Spinning Wheel Dr., Suite 416
Hinsdale, IL 60521
(708) 858-1649
Parent advocacy group.

The Self-Help Center
1600 Dodge Ave.
Evanston, IL 60201
(800) 322-6274

INDIANA

Indiana Alliance for the Mentally Ill
P.O. Box 22697
Indianapolis, IN 46222-0697
(317) 236-0056
(317) 236-8166 (Fax)

Indiana Youth Institute
3901 N. Meridian St., Suite 200
Indianapolis, IN 46208-4046
(800) 343-7060
(317) 924-3657
(317) 924-1314 (Fax)
http://www.iyi.org/iyi (Internet)

KEY Consumer Organization
210 N. Warman Ave.
Indianapolis, IN 46222
(317) 686-6074

Koala Behavioral Health Network
1711 Lafayette Ave.
Lebanon, IN 46052
(800) 562-5215

IOWA

Alliance for the Mentally Ill of Iowa
5911 Meredith Dr., Suite C-1
Des Moines, IA 50322-1903
(800) 417-0417
(515) 254-1103 (Fax)

Iowa Pilot Parents
P.O. Box 1151
Fort Dodge, IA 50501
(800) 952-4777
Parent training and information center for parents of
children with special needs

Iowa Coalition
1251 334th St.
Woodward, IA 50276
(800) 775-2379
Statewide advocacy organization of and for mental
health consumer/advocates promotes self-help and
assistance in areas such as education, employment,
housing, and mental health services. Services available include meetings and forums, lending library,
newsletter, speakers bureau, support groups, and job
training and public education programs.

Iowa Federation of Families for Children's Mental Health
13276 Circle Dr.
Anamosa, IA 52205
(319) 462-4423
Parent advocacy group.

Mental Health Consumer Resource Project
Hoover State Office Bldg., 5th Floor
Des Moines, IA 50319
(515) 281-7274
Collaborative effort between the Iowa Department of Human Services and the Iowa Coalition designed to give mental health consumers a voice in policymaking at the state level. Project provides technical assistance to consumer groups throughout the state, participates in the development of state mental health planning, and educates the public about consumer issues.

KANSAS

Advocates for Freedom in Mental Health
1026 South 56th Terrace
Kansas City, KS 66106

Kansas Alliance for the Mentally Ill
112 SW 6th, P.O. Box 675
Topeka, KS 66601-0675
(913) 233-0755
(913) 233-4804 (Fax)

Mental Health Association for Central Kansas
555 N. Woodlawn, Suite 3105
Witchita, KS 67208
(316) 685-1821

Sedgwick County Federation of Families for Children's Mental Health
555 North Woodlawn, #3105
Witchita, KS 67208
(316) 264-3016
(316) 685-0768 (Fax)
Parent advocacy group.

Self-Help Network
Wichita State University
Box 34, 1845 Fairmount
Wichita, KA 67260
(316) 978-3843
(800) 445-0116

KENTUCKY

F.A.C.E.S of the Bluegrass
570 East Main St.
Lexington, KY 40508
(606) 266-3236
Parent advocacy group.

Kentucky Alliance for the Mentally Ill
10510 LaGrange Rd., Bldg. 103
Louisville, KY 40223-1228
(502) 245-5284
(502) 245-5287 (Fax)

Kentucky IMPACT
275 E. Main St.
Frankfort, KY 40621
(502) 564-7610
Parent advocacy group.

Project Vision
2210 Goldsmith Lane, #118
Louisville, KY 40218
(800) 525-7746
(502) 456-0893 (Fax)
Parent advocacy group.

S.P.O.K.E.S.
275 E. Main St.
Frankfort, KY 40621
(502) 564-7610
(502) 564-9010 (Fax)
Parent advocacy group.

LOUISIANA

Louisiana Alliance for the Mentally Ill
  P.O. Box 2547
  Baton Rouge, LA 70821-2547
  (504) 343-6928
  (504) 388-9133 (Fax)
  Support and advocacy organization sponsors local
  support groups and offers education and information
  about community services for people with mental illness and their families.

Louisiana Federation of Families for Children's Mental
Health
  920 Pierremont Rd., Suite 308
  Shreveport, LA 71106
  (800) 224-4010
  Parent advocacy group.

Louisiana Organization of Child and Adolescent
Psychiatry
  LSU Medical School
  1542 Tulane Ave., Room A328
  New Orleans, LA 70112-2822
  (504) 568-3031

MAINE

Alliance for the Mentally Ill of Maine
  P.O. Box 222
  Augusta, ME 04332-0222
  (800) 464-5767
  (202) 622-5767 (Fax)
  Support and advocacy organization sponsors local
  support groups and offers education and information
  about community services for people with mental illness and their families.

Maine Organization of Child and Adolescent Psychiatry
  172 Maine St.
  Brunswick, ME 04011-2036
  (207) 729-8391

MARYLAND

Alliance for the Mentally Ill of Maryland Inc.
  711 W. 40th St., Suite 451
  Baltimore, MD 21211
  (410) 889-4878
  (410) 467-7195 (Fax)
  Support and advocacy organization sponsors local
  support groups and offers education and information
  about community services for people with mental illness and their families.

Greater Washington DC Self-Help Clearinghouse
  Mental Health Association of Northern Virginia
  7630 Little River Tpke., Suite 206
  Annandale, VA 22003
  (703) 941-5465
  Provides information on self-help/support groups for
  the Washington, DC, Metropolitan area.

Maryland Organization of Child and Adolescent
Psychiatry
  CMSC 314 Johns Hopkins Hospital
  600 N. Wolfe St.
  Baltimore, MD 21205
  (410) 955-7025

Montgomery County Federation of Families for
Children's Mental Health
  17717 Cliffbourne Lane
  Derwood, MD 20855
  (301) 963-0625
  Parent advocacy group.

Parents Supporting Parents
  4012 Byrd Rd.
  Kensington, MD 20895
  (301) 949-4352
  Parent advocacy group.

Tri-County Youth Services Bureau
  P.O. Box 400
  Charlotte Hall, MD 20622
  (301) 274-3105
  (301) 884-5406 (Fax)
  Serves children, adolescents, and their families in
  Charles, Calvert, and St. Mary's counties.

Youth Crisis Hotline - Maryland
(800) 422-0009
Trained listeners provide information, referrals, and counseling to both youth and adults. This is a state hotline in which designated counties intercept calls.

MASSACHUSETTS

Alliance for the Mentally Ill of Massachusetts Inc.
295 Devonshire St.
Boston, MA 02110-1625
(800) 370-9085
(617) 426-0088 (Fax)

Massachusetts Clearinghouse of Mutual Help Groups
University of Massachusetts
113 Skinner Hall
Amherst, MA 01003
(413) 545-2313
Provides information on self-help/support groups in Massachusetts.

Parent Professional Advocacy League
95 Berkeley St., Suite 104
Boston, MA 02116-6237
(800) 331-0688
(617) 695-2939 (Fax)
Parent advocacy group.

Roxbury United for Families and Children
85 E. Newton St., #839
Boston, MA 02118
(617) 236-4744
(617) 867-9114 (Fax)
Parent advocacy group.

MICHIGAN

Alliance for the Mentally Ill of Michigan
921 N. Washington
Lansing, MI 48906
(800) 331-4264

Association for Children's Mental Health
1705 Coolidge Rd.
Woodbrook Village #2
East Lansing, MI 48823
(517) 336-7222
Parent advocacy group.

Center for Self-Help
Riverwood Center
P.O. Box 541
Benton Harbor, MI 49022
(616) 925-0585

Michigan Advocacy
106 W. Allegan, Suite 300
Lansing, MI 48933
(517) 487-1755

Michigan Association for Children with Emotional Disorders
15920 W. Twelve Mile Rd., Suite 201
Southfield, MI 48076
(810) 552-0044
(810) 552-0047 (Fax)
Parent advocacy group.

Michigan Clearinghouse
106 W. Allegan, Suite 210
Lansing, MI 48933
(800) 777-5556
Provides information on self-help/support groups in Michigan.

MINNESOTA

Alliance for the Mentally Ill of Minnesota, Inc.
970 Raymond Ave., Suite 105
St. Paul, MN 55114-1146
(612) 645-2948
(612) 645-7379 (Fax)

Consumer Network Line
1821 University Ave. West, Suite N178
Saint Paul, MN 55104
(800) 483-2007

First Call for Help
166 East 4th St., Suite 310
St. Paul, MN 55101
(612) 224-1133
Minnesota Association for Children's Mental Health
1498 Clemson St.
Egan, MN 55122
(612) 644-7333
Parent advocacy group.

Pacer Center, Inc.
4826 Chicago Ave. South
Minneapolis, MN 55417
(612) 827-2966

MISSISSIPPI

Mental Health Association
5135 Galaxie Dr., Suite 501E
Jackson, MS 39206
(601) 982-4003
(601) 982-4059 (Fax)

Mississippi Alliance for the Mentally Ill
5135 Galaxie Dr., Suite 503E
Jackson, MS 39206
(601) 981-4491

Mississippi Families as Allies
5166 Keele St., Suite B-100
Jackson, MS 39206
(601) 981-1618
(601) 981-1696 (Fax)
Parent advocacy group.

Mississippi Mental Health Consumers Coalition
155 Pleasant Ct.
Jackson, MS 39203
(601) 352-5674

MISSOURI

Missouri Clearinghouse - St. Louis
1905 South Grand
St. Louis, MO 63104
(314) 773-1399

Provides information on self-help/support groups for the St. Louis area.

Missouri Coalition of the Alliance for the Mentally Ill
230 W. Dunklin St., Room 204
Jefferson City, MO 65101-3260
(800) 374-2138
(314) 634-7727 (Fax)

Missouri Mental Health Consumer Network
P.O. Box 297
Jefferson City, MO 65109
(800) 359-5695
(573) 526-3503

Missouri Organization of Child and Adolescent Psychiatry
11906 Manchester Rd., Suite 205
St. Louis, MO 63131-4505
(314) 822-9222

The Self-Help Center
212 North Kirkwood Rd.
Kirkwood, MO 63122
(314) 966-4980

MO-SPAN
1124 Bliss Dr.
St. Louis, MO 63137
(314) 388-3180
(314) 388-3189 (Fax)
Parent advocacy group.

MONTANA

Family Support Network
P.O. Box 21366
Billings, MT 59104
(406) 256-7783
(406) 256-9879 (Fax)
Parent advocacy group.

MONAMI (Montana Alliance for the Mentally Ill)
P.O. Box 1021
Helena, MT 59624
(406) 443-7871
(406) 443-1592 (Fax)

NEBRASKA

Nebraska Alliance for the Mentally Ill for Greater
Omaha
    4001 Leavenworth
    Omaha, NE 68105
    (402) 341-5128

Nebraska Clearinghouse
    (402) 476-9668
    Provides information on self-help/support groups in
    Nebraska.

Nebraska Organization of Child and Adolescent
Psychiatry
    9818 Westchester Dr.
    Omaha, NE 68114
    (402) 449-5144

NE Family Support Network
    215 Centennial Mall South, Room 220
    Lincoln, NE 68508-1813
    (402) 477-2992
    (402) 477-8317 (Fax)
    melaniek@del.com (e-mail)
    Parent advocacy group.

NEVADA

Alliance for the Mentally Ill of Nevada
    2600 Spinaker Dr.
    Reno, NV 89509
    (702) 825-7023
    (702) 825-3965 (Fax)

Nevada Disabilities Advocacy and Law Center
    410 S. Third St., Suite 403
    Las Vegas, NV 89101
    (702) 333-7878
    State protection and advocacy agency.

NEW HAMPSHIRE

Alliance for the Mentally Ill of New Hampshire
    10 Ferry St., Unit 314
    Concord, NH 03301-5004
    (603) 225-5359

Consumer Support Center
    1145 Sagamore Ave.
    Portsmouth, NH 03801
    (603) 427-6966

New Hampshire Disabilities Rights Center, Inc.
    18 Low Ave.
    P.O. Box 19
    Concord, NH 03302
    (800) 852-3336
    (603) 225-2077 (Fax)

NEW JERSEY

Coalition of Mental Health Consumer Organizations
    67 Marine Terrace, Apt. 3
    Long Branch, NJ 05540
    (908) 870-9018

New Jersey Alliance for the Mentally Ill
    200 West State St., 3rd Floor
    Trenton, NJ 08608-1102
    (609) 695-4554
    (609) 695-0908 (Fax)

New Jersey Self-Help Clearinghouse
    Northwest Covenant Medical Center
    25 Pocono Rd.
    Denville, NJ 07834
    (201) 625-9565
    (800) 367-6274
    Provides information on self-help/support groups in
    New Jersey.

New Jersey Organization of Child and Adolescent
Psychiatry
    111 Dean Dr.
    Tenafly, NJ 07670-2708
    (201) 567-3112

New Jersey Protection and Advocacy Inc.
210 South Broad St., 3rd Floor
Trenton, NJ 08608
(609) 292-9742
(609) 777-0187 (Fax)
State protection and advocacy agency.

NEW MEXICO

Alliance for the Mentally Ill of New Mexico
1720 Louisiana Blvd. NE, Suite 214
Albuquerque, NM 87110
(505) 254-0643
(505) 254-0674 (Fax)

NAMI/New Mexico Consumer Council
P.O. Box 31
Serafina, NM 87569
(505) 843-6265

Parents for Behaviorally Different Children
7732 Hermanson, NE
Albuquerque, NM 87110
(505) 265-0430
Parent advocacy group.

Ponderosa Child Development Center
5301 Ponderosa, NE
Albuquerque, NM 87110
(505) 881-4331
Day care provider for children with disabilities.

NEW YORK

Alliance for the Mentally Ill of New York State
260 Washington Ave.
Albany, NY 12210-1312
(800) 950-3228
(518) 462-3811 (Fax)

Client Support Network
Sunnyside Reformed Church
48-03 Skillman Ave.
Long Island City, NY 11104
(212) 684-3264

McQuade Children's Services
P.O. Box 4064
New Windsor, NY 12553
(914) 561-0436
Provides a wide range of services to children in New York State including residential treatment, day treatment, schooling, group homes, diagnostic shelter, prevention programs, independent living programs, court-related services, and foster homes. It also makes referrals to other social service and support organizations.

Mental Health Association
169 Central Ave.
Albany, NY 12206
(518) 434-0439
(518) 427-8676 (Fax)

Mental Health Association of New York City
666 Broadway, 2nd Floor
New York, NY 10012
(212) 254-0333

New York (Capitol) Organization of Child and Adolescent Psychiatry
44 East Bayberry Rd.
Glenmount, NY 12077-3027
(518) 447-9665

New York City Self-Help Center
New York, NY
(212) 586-5770
Provides information on self-help/support groups for the New York City area.

New York - Westchester Jewish Family SVS Self-Help Clearinghouse
456 N. St.
White Plains, NY 10605
(914) 949-0788
Provides information on self-help/support groups in the Westchester area.

NORTH CAROLINA

Families CAN
  3820 Bland Rd.
  Raleigh, NC 27609
  (919) 790-9500
  (800) 211-0501
  Provides advocacy, support and information for families of children and adolescents with emotional and behavioral disorders and mental illnesses.

North Carolina Alliance for the Mentally Ill
  4904 Waters Edge Dr., Suite 152
  Raleigh, NC 27606
  (919) 851-0063
  (919) 851-5989 (Fax)

North Carolina Mental Health Consumers' Organization
  P.O. Box 27042
  Raleigh, NC 27611-7042
  (800) 326-3842

SupportWorks
  1018 East Blvd.
  Charlotte, NC
  (704) 331-9500
  Provides information on self-help/support groups in North Carolina.

NORTH DAKOTA

Harmony Center
  212 E. Central Ave.
  Minot, ND 58701
  (701) 852-3263
  Resources and support for people with mental illness.

North Dakota Alliance for the Mentally Ill
  1809 S. Broadway, Unit H
  Minot, ND 58701
  (701) 838-0166
  (701) 852-1742 (Fax)

North Dakota Federation of Families for Children's Mental Health
  706 N. Third St.
  Bismarck, ND 58501
  (701) 258-1921
  (701) 328-2359 (Fax)
  Parent advocacy group.

OHIO

Alliance for the Mentally Ill of Ohio
  979 S. High St.
  Columbus, OH 43206-2525
  (800) 686-2646
  (614) 445-6503 (Fax)

Child and Adolescent Network - AMI of Toledo
  1 Stranahan Square, Suite 560
  Toledo, OH 43604
  (419) 243-1119

Child and Adolescent Service Center
  919 Second St. NE
  Canton, OH 44704
  (330) 454-7917
  Parent advocacy services.

Ohio (Cincinnati) Organization of Child and Adolescent Psychiatry
  Dept. of Psychiatry
  Wright State University
  P.O. Box 927
  Dayton, OH 45401-0927
  (513) 276-8325

Ohio Clearinghouse - Dayton area
  Dayton, OH
  (513) 225-3004
  Provides information on self-help/support groups in the Dayton area.

Ohio Harbour Behavior Center
  4334 Secour Rd.
  Toledo, OH 43623
  (419) 475-4449
  Provides information on self-help/support groups in the Toledo area.

Ohio (Northeast) Organization of Child and Adolescent Psychiatry
  Cleveland Clinic
  One Clinic Center
  Cleveland, OH 44195-0001
  (216) 444-2820

Specialized Alternatives for Families and Youth of America (SAFY)
  10100 Elida Rd.
  Delphos, OH 45833
  (800) 532-7239

OKLAHOMA

Child and Adolescent Network
  200 NW 66th, #925
  Oklahoma City, OK 73116
  (800) 583-1264
  (405) 848-4330 (Fax)

Lauriet Psychiatric Hospital
  6655 South Yale
  Tulsa, OK 74136-3329
  (918) 481-4000

Oklahoma Alliance for the Mentally Ill
  200 NW 66th St., Suite 925
  Oklahoma City, OK 73116
  (800) 583-1264
  (405) 848-4330 (Fax)

Oklahoma Mental Health Consumer Council
  1211 SW 59th St.
  Oklahoma City, OK 73109
  (405) 634-5644
  (405) 634-2075 (Fax)
  Advocacy organization for consumers has membership of 1,500 within the state. Provides brochures and information on mental illnesses, as well as referral service for medication, community mental health centers, legal centers, and vocational rehab services for people with mental illness. Responds to the general public on mental health issues.

OREGON

Metro Consumer Network
  5120 Southeast 28th
  Portland, OR 97202

Options for Southern Oregon
  202 NW A St.
  Grants Pass, OR 97526
  (541) 476-2373

Oregon Advocacy Center
  620 SW Fifth Ave., Suite 500
  Portland, OR 97204-1428
  (503) 243-2081
  (503) 243-1738 (Fax)
  State protection and advocacy agency.

Oregon Alliance for the Mentally Ill
  161 High St. SE, Suite 212
  Salem, OR 97301-3610
  (503) 370-7774
  (503) 370-9452 (Fax)

Oregon Family Support Network Inc.
  P.O. Box 13820
  Salem, OR 97309
  (503) 581-2047
  (503) 581-4841 (Fax)
  Parent advocacy group.

United Way Info Referrals
  P.O. Box 637
  Portland, OR 97207
  (503) 222-5555
  Provides information on self-help/support groups in Oregon.

PENNSYLVANIA

Alliance for the Mentally Ill of Pennsylvania
  2149 N. 2nd St.
  Harrisburg, PA 17110-1005
  (800) 223-0500
  (717) 238-4390 (Fax)

State Mental Health Organizations

F.I.R.S.T.
Scranton Life Bldg., Suite 420
538 Spruce St.
Scranton, PA 18503
(717) 961-1234
Provides information on self-help/support groups in
the Scranton area.

Mental Health Association
311 S. Juniper St.
Philadelphia, PA 19107
(215) 751-1800

Pennsylvania Mental Health Consumers Association
108 E. Walnut St.
Lancaster, PA 17602
(800) 887-6422

Pennsylvania Protection and Advocacy, Inc.
116 Pine St., Suite 102
Harrisburg, PA 17101
(717) 236-8110
(717) 236-0192 (Fax)
State protection and advocacy agency.

Pennsylvania Self-Help Group Network Clearinghouse -
Pittsburgh area
1323 Forbes Ave.
Pittsburgh, PA 15219
(412) 261-5363
Provides information on self-help/support groups in
the Pittsburgh area.

Psychiatric Facility
Philhaven Hospital
283 S. Butler Rd.
Mt. Gretna, PA 17064-9999
(717) 273-8871

Special Kids Network
P.O. Box 850
Hershey, PA 17033-0850
(717) 531-4848
(717) 531-5878 (Fax)
Provides information and referrals to parents of children with special needs and health care providers who
treat this population. A call to the central number
puts people in touch with a center in their region of

the state where they can find out about local and
statewide health and social services.

PUERTO RICO

Associacion de Padres pro Bienestar de Ninos con
Impedimentos (APNI)
P.O. Box 21301
San Juan, PR 00928
(809) 763-4665
(809) 765-0345 (Fax)
Parent advocacy group.

Puerto Rico Organization of Child and Adolescent
Psychiatry
Calle A #34 Vistapoint
Ponce, PR 00731
(809) 848-2615

RHODE ISLAND

Alliance for the Mentally Ill of Rhode Island
P.O. Box 28411
Providence, RI 02908-0411
(401) 464-3060
(401) 464-1686 (Fax)
Support and advocacy organization sponsors local
support groups and offers education and information
about community services for people with mental illness and their families.

Coalition of Consumer Self-Advocates
P.O. Box 8446
Cottage 402
Cranston, RI 02920
(401) 464-2231
(401) 464-1564 (Fax)

Parent Support Network
2905 Post Rd.
Warwick, RI 02886
(401) 736-8844
(800) 483-8844
(401) 738-8485 (Fax)
Parent advocacy group.

Rhode Island Protection and Advocacy System, Inc.
  151 Broadway, 3rd Floor
  Providence, RI 02903
  (401) 831-3150
  (401) 274-5568 (Fax)
  State protection and advocacy agency.

SOUTH CAROLINA

Charleston Dorchester Community Mental Health
Center
  1 Carriage Lane, Bldg. G
  Charleston,SC 29407
  (803) 852-4125
  (803) 852-4130 (Fax)
  Parent advocacy group.

South Carolina Alliance for the Mentally Ill
  P.O. Box 2538
  Columbia, SC 29202-2538
  (803) 779-7849
  (803) 779-7849 (Fax)
  Support and advocacy organization sponsors local
  support groups and offers education and information
  about community services for people with mental illness and their families.

Support Group - Lexington Medical Center
  2720 Sunset Blvd.
  West Colum, SC 29169
  (803) 791-9227
  Provides information on self-help/support groups in
  South Carolina.

SOUTH DAKOTA

Child Psychiatry
  USD Medical School
  1100 S. Euclid
  P.O. Box 5039
  Sioux Falls, SD 57117-5039
  (605) 333-7198

Mental Health Outreach Network
  P.O. Box 732
  Lead, SD 57754
  (605) 355-2274

South Dakota Alliance for the Mentally Ill
  P.O. Box 221
  Brookings, SD 57006
  (800) 551-2531
  (605) 692-6132 (Fax)

TENNESSEE

Mental Health Association
  2400 Poplar Ave., Suite 410
  Memphis, TN 37112
  (901) 323-0633

Pine Point Center
  49 Old Hickory Blvd.
  Jackson, TN 38301-7301
  (800) 336-1544
  Rehabilitation program for children and adolescents

Tennessee Mental Health Consumers Association
  1323 Caney Valley Loop
  Sugoinsville, TN 37873
  (800) 459-2925

Tennessee Mental Health Organization
  P.O. Box 121257
  Nashville, TN 37212
  (800) 342-1660
  (615) 298-2046 (Fax)

Tennessee Self-Help Clearinghouse
  Memphis Mental Health Association
  2400 Poplar Ave., Suite 410
  Memphis, TN 37112
  (901) 323-0633
  Provides information on self-help/support groups in
  Tennessee.

Tennessee Voices for Children
  2200 21st Ave., South 109
  Nashville, TN 37212
  (615) 269-7751

State Mental Health Organizations

TEXAS

Houston Advocates for Mentally Ill Children
24 Greenway Plaza, Suite 1100
Houston, TX 77046
(713) 783-8470

Parent Connection
1020 Riverwood Ct.
Conroe, TX 77304
(409) 525-2746
parent@neosoft.com (e-mail)

Special Kids Inc.
6202 Belmark
Houston, TX 77087
(713) 734-5355

Texas Alliance for the Mentally Ill
1000 East 7th St., Suite 208
Austin, TX 78702-3257
(512) 474-2225
(512) 320-0887 (Fax)
Support and advocacy organization sponsors local
support groups and offers education and information
about community services for people with mental illness and their families.

Texas Federation of Families for Children's Mental
Health
Parent Connection
1020 Riverwood Ct.
Conroe, TX 77304
(409) 525-2746
patti.derr@mmp.org (e-mail)
Parent advocacy group.

Texas Mental Health Consumers
101 West 6th St., Suite 601
Austin, TX 78701
(512) 451-3191

Texas Self-Help Clearinghouse
840 Shoal Creek Blvd.
Austin, TX 78757
(512) 454-3706
Provides information on self-help/support groups in
Texas.

UTAH

Information and Referral Center
1025 S. 700 West
Salt Lake City, UT 84106
(801) 978-3333

Intermountain Organization of Child and Adolescent
Psychiatry
732 N. Richland Dr.
Salt Lake City, UT 84103
(801) 588-3576

Parents Center
2290 East 4500 South, Suite 110
Salt Lake City, UT 84117
(800) 468-1160
(801)272-8907 (Fax)
Parent advocacy group works with parents who have
children with behavioral and neurobiological disabilities by providing referrals and information.

Utah Alliance for the Mentally Ill
P.O. Box 58047
Salt Lake City, UT 84158-0047
(801) 584-2023
(801) 582-8471 (Fax)
Support and advocacy organization sponsors local
support groups and offers education and information
about community services for people with mental illness and their families.

VERMONT

Alliance for the Mentally Ill of Vermont
230 Main St., Room 203
Brattleboro, VT 05301-2840
(802) 257-5546
(802) 257-5886 (Fax)

Center for Children and Families
One S. Prospect St.
Burlington, VT 05401-3444
(802) 656-4563

Vermont Association for Mental Health
P.O. Box 165
Montpelier, VT 05601
(802) 223-6263

Vermont Federation of Families for Children's Mental Health
P.O. Box 607
Montpelier, VT 05601-0607
(802) 223-4917
(802) 229-9233 (Fax)
Parent advocacy group.

Vermont Protection and Advocacy
21 East State St., Suite 101
Montpelier, VT 05602
(802) 229-1355
(802) 229-1359 (Fax)

VIRGINIA

Dept. of Rights for Virginians with Disabilities
202 N. Ninth St. Office Bldg., 9th Floor
Richmond, VA 23219
(800) 552-3962
(804) 225-3221 (Fax)
State protection and advocacy agency.

Federation of Families for Children's Health
1021 Prince St.
Alexandria, VA 22314
(703) 684-7710

Greater Washington DC Self-Help Clearinghouse
Mental Health Association of Northern Virginia
7630 Little River Tpke., Suite 206
Annandale, VA 22003
(703) 941-5465
Provides information on self-help/support groups for the Washington, DC, Metropolitan area.

Parents & Children Coping Together
201 W. Broad St., Suite 503
Richmond, VA 23220-4216
(804) 225-0002

Virginia Alliance for the Mentally Ill
P.O. Box 1903
Richmond, VA 23215-1903
(804) 225-8264
(804) 643-3632 (Fax)
Support and advocacy organization sponsors local support groups and offers education and information about community services for people with mental illness and their families.

Virginia Board of Psychology
(804) 662-9913

Virginia Mental Health Consumers Association
1111 N. Thompson St.
Richmond, VA 23230
(800) 352-7381
(804) 359-8298 (Fax)
Network of individuals and groups empowers mental health consumers and advocate for change. The association educates and empowers consumers to address their own issues surrounding care, treatment, and services and to preserve the respect, dignity, and human rights of mental health consumers. The association also works to eliminate the stigma surrounding mental illness by educating the public.

The Women's Center
133 Park St., NE
Vienna, VA 22180
(703) 281-2657
Regional resource for women, children, and families provides psychotherapy, support and therapy groups, separation and divorce counseling, personal growth and family strengthening workshops, career services, and financial education.

WASHINGTON

State of Washington Alliance for the Mentally Ill
2562 Norway Drive
Ferndale, WA 98248
(360) 380-7347
(360) 380-7347 (Fax)
Support and advocacy organization offers education and information about community services for people with mental illness and their families.

Washington Organization of Child and Adolescent Psychiatry
23101 30th Ave. NE, Suite B-202
Bellevue, WA 98005-1757
(206) 455-1650

Washington State Protection and Advocacy Agency.
1401 E. Jefferson St., Suite 506
Seattle, WA 98122
(206) 324-1521
(206) 324-1783 (Fax)
State protection and advocacy agency.

WEST VIRGINIA

Mountain State Parents, Children, and Adolescents Network
20 Richmond Ave.
Wheeling, WV 26003
(800) 244-5385
Parent advocacy group.

West Virginia Advocates
1207 Quarrier St., 4th Floor
Charleston, WV 25311
(800) 950-5250
(304) 346-0867 (Fax)
State protection and advocacy agency.

West Virginia Alliance for the Mentally Ill
P.O. Box 2706
Charleston, WV 25330-2706
(304) 342-0497
(304) 342-0499 (Fax)
Support and advocacy organization sponsors local support groups and offers education and information about community services for people with mental illness and their families.

West Virginia Mental Health Consumers Association
184 Summers St.
Charleston, WV 25301
(800) 598-8847
(304)345-7303 (Fax)

WISCONSIN

Alliance for the Mentally Ill of Wisconsin Inc.
1410 Northport Dr.
Madison, WI 53704-2041
(608) 242-7223

Mental Health Association - Milwaukee
734 N. 4th St., Suite 325
Milwaukee, WI 53403
(414) 276-3122

Peer Connection
P.O. Box 9301
Madison, WI 53715-0301
(608) 258-9848

Wisconsin Coalition for Advocacy Inc.
16 N. Carroll St., Suite 400
Madison, WI 53703
(608) 267-0214
(608) 267-0368 (Fax)
State protection and advocacy agency.

Wisconsin Family Ties, Inc.
16 N. Carroll St., Suite 630
Madison, WI 53703
(608) 267-6888
(608) 267-6801 (Fax)
Parent advocacy group.

Wisconsin Network of Mental Health Consumers
Route 3, Box 404
Ashland, WI 54806

Wisconsin Organization of Child and Adolescent Psychiatry
2000 W. Kilbourn
Milwaukee, WI 53233-1625
(414) 937-5492

WYOMING

Family Alliance for the Mentally Ill
100 W. B
Casper, WY 82601
(307) 234-0440

Protection and Advocacy System Inc.
  2424 Pioneer Ave., Suite 101
  Cheyenne, WY 82001
  (800) 624-7648
  (307) 638-0815 (Fax)
  State protection and advocacy agency.

UPLIFT
  P.O. Box 664
  Cheyenne, WY 82003-0664
  (307) 778-8686
  Parent advocacy group provides information, referrals, and one-on-one advocacy for parents with children who have emotional, mental, and behavioral problems.

Wyoming Alliance for the Mentally Ill
  656 Granite Dr.
  Rock Springs, WY 82901
  (307) 362-3333
  Support and advocacy organization sponsors local support groups and offers education and information about community services for people with mental illness and their families.

Wyoming Parent Information Center
  5 N. Luban
  Buffalo, WY 82834
  (307) 684-2277
  Parent advocacy group.

Americans with Disabilities Act (ADA): The ADA details requirements for disabled persons regarding, employment, transportation, public accommodations, state and local government, and telecommunications. Under Title III of the ADA, new construction and alterations of commercial facilities must comply fully with ADA Accessibility Guidelines. Included in "public accommodations" are places of education (i.e., preschool, nursery, elementary, secondary, undergraduate or post graduate private school). Any private entity that owns, leases, leases to, or operates an existing public accommodation must comply with four specific requirements:

1. Remove barriers to make their goods and services available to and usable by people with disabilities, to the extent that it is readily achievable to do so—in other words, to the extent that needed changes can be accomplished without much difficulty or expense.

2. Provide auxiliary aids and services so that people with sensory or cognitive disabilities have access to effective means of communication, unless doing so would fundamentally alter the operation or result in undue burdens.

3. Modify any policies, practices, or procedures that may be discriminatory or have a discriminatory effect, unless doing so would fundamentally alter the nature of the goods, services, facilities, or accommodations.

4. Ensure that there are no unnecessary eligibility criteria that tend to screen out or segregate individuals with disabilities or limit their full and equal enjoyment of the place of public accommodation.

FEDERAL EDUCATION LEGISLATION

Individuals with Disabilities Education Act (IDEA): This legislation was enacted in 1975 in response to the widespread exclusion of children with disabilities (mental and/or physical) from educational programs that would meet their individual special needs. IDEA mandates that every child, regardless of disability, be provided with a free and appropriate public education which will meet his or her unique needs.

The main requirements which IDEA places upon the states and local school systems include mandates to:

• Identify and evaluate children with disabilities.
• Develop for each student with an identified disability an Individualized Education Program (IEP) designed to meet his or her unique needs.
• Periodically review the effectiveness and appropriateness of the IEP.
• Provide specific procedures for parents who wish to challenge the appropriateness or adequacy of the educational services being provided for their child.

As of the beginning of April 1996, the Senate Labor and Human Resources Committee had unanimously approved the proposed revisions to IDEA (Senate Bill S.1578), and the Senate was readying itself to vote on it. Of particular concern to advocates for children with disabilities is the opposition to reauthorizing the provisions of IDEA which inform the disciplinary procedures to be used with students with disabilities. More specifically, IDEA endorses "stay put" rules which outline specific procedures school officials must follow before expelling or placing on long-term suspension a student with a disability. These rules are particularly important for protecting the rights of these students who are often labeled as "trouble-makers" or "problem" students. According to the Bazelon Center for Mental Health Law, the suspension and expulsion rates for the same misbehaviors is twice as high for students with disabilities than for their nondisabled peers.

Opponents to the reauthorization of these "stay put" rules contend that the authority of school officials to use their own judgment in making disciplinary decisions is severely and unfairly diminished by these provisions.

The new disciplinary provisions contained in S.1578 would allow schools and school officials to:

• Suspend or change the educational placement of students for up to 10 school days even if the misbehavior was related to the student's disability.
• Decide if the misbehavior was related to or a result of the student's disability (called a "manifestation hearing") when the disciplinary action extends beyond 10 days.
• Provide parents with an opportunity to challenge the determination of the manifestation hearing by requesting an expedited due process hearing during which time the

student would remain at his or her current school placement until a ruling is rendered.

• Place for up to 35 school days students who possessed weapons or drugs, seriously injured someone, or engaged in "serious disruptive behavior" regardless of whether the misbehaviors resulted from the student's disability (in this case, the student would remain in alternative placement even during due process hearing).

The new term "serious disruptive behavior" is qualified only by describing it as behavior which "significantly impairs the education of the student or other students and the ability of the teacher to teach." The term is left otherwise undefined by the bill, and advocates are concerned that this would allow school officials too much unbridled discretion in determining what constitutes serious disruptive behavior. Although parents are afforded the right to challenge the decision, in the interim, students with disabilities who already are multiply challenged are subject to the additional chaos, confusion, and stress of being forced into another setting for up to seven school weeks. This potentially traumatic disruption may ultimately be determined by a hearing officer to be ill-advised or unjustified.

The following eight pieces of federal legislation require school officials to know and be familiar with existing education pedagogies and to determine which to implement in their local schools in order to most effectively empower the system to meet the needs of students.

1. **Chapter One of the Elementary and Secondary Education Act of 1965:** This act's overall purpose is to make funds available to state educational agencies to "provide programs that supplement services to children who are disabled and enrolled in State operated or State supported schools and programs to children who are disabled and enrolled in local educational agencies that have transferred from a State school or program." (A Catalog of Federal Domestic Assistance, #84.009)

"A local educational agency may use funds received under this part only for programs which are designed to meet the...educational needs of educationally deprived ...Each application shall provide assurance that the programs and projects described are of sufficient size, scope, and quality to give reasonable promise of progress toward meeting the...educational needs of the children..."

2. **The Education of All Handicapped Children Act:** "Each (state and local) plan shall set forth, consistent with the purposes of this chapter, a description of programs and procedures for (A) the development and implementation of a comprehensive system of personnel development which shall include the in-service training of general and special educational instructional and support personnel..., and effective procedures for acquiring and disseminating to teachers and administrators...significant information derived from educational research, demonstration, and similar projects, and (B) adopting, where appropriate, promising educational practices and materials develop(ed) through such projects."

3. **The Carl D. Perkins Vocational and Applied Technology Act of 1990:** Overall purpose: "To make the United States more competitive in the world economy by developing more fully the academic and occupational skills of all segments of the population, principally through concentrating resources on improving educational programs leading to academic and occupational skills needed to work in a technologically advanced society." (A Catalog of Federal Domestic Assistance, #84.048)

"Funds made available under a grant under this part shall be used to provide vocational education in programs that (A) are of such size, scope, and quality as to be effective; (B) integrate academic and vocational education in such programs through coherent sequences of courses so that students achieve both academic and occupational competencies."

4. **The Bilingual Education Act:** "The programs assisted under this subchapter include programs in elementary and secondary schools as well as related preschool and adult programs which are designed to meet the educational needs of individuals of limited English proficiency, with particular attention to children having the greatest need for such programs. Such programs shall be designed to enable students to achieve full competence in English and to meet school grade-promotion and graduation requirements."

5. **The Migrant Education Act:** "The Secretary may approve an application submitted under...this title only upon a determination...that payments will be used for programs and projects...which are designed to meet the special educational needs of migratory children of migratory agricultural workers...or of migratory fishermen..."

6. **The Head Start Act:** "The Secretary may, upon application by an agency which is eligible for designation as a Head Start agency...provide financial assistance to such agency for the planning, conduct, administration, and evaluation of a Head Start program focused primarily upon children from low-income families who have not reached the age of compulsory school attendance which (1) will provide such comprehensive health, nutritional, educational, social, and other services as will aid the children to attain their full potential; and (2) will provide for direct participation of the parents of such children in the development, conduct, and overall program direction at the local level."

7. **The Early Education of Handicapped Children Act:** Overall purpose: "To support demonstration, dissemination, and implementation of effective approaches to preschool and early childhood education for children with disabilities." (A Catalog of Federal Domestic Assistance, #84.024)

"The Secretary shall make a grant to any State which...has a State plan approved under section 1413 (including the requirement for adopting promising educational practices quoted above at n. 3) of this title which includes policies and procedures that assure the availability under the State law and practice of such State of a free appropriate public education for all handicapped children ages 3 to 5, inclusive...

"The Secretary may arrange by contract, grant, or cooperative agreement with appropriate public agencies and private nonprofit organizations, for the development and operation of experimental, demonstration, and outreach preschool and early intervention programs for handicapped children which...(D) offer training about exemplary models and practices to State and local personnel who provide services to handicapped children from birth through age 8, and (E) support the adoption of exemplary models and practices in States and local communities."

8. **National Diffusion Network Act:** Overall purpose: "To identify, validate, and disseminate effective schoolwide projects and programs addressing the needs of high poverty schools, and programs with the capacity to offer high-quality, sustained technical assistance for adoption by public and nonpublic educational institutions." (A Catalog of Federal Domestic Assistance, #84.073)

"The National Diffusion Network shall be designed to improve the quality of education through the implementation of promising and validated innovations and improvements in educational programs, products, and practices, and through the provision of training, consultation, and related assistance services.

"The Secretary shall (1) acquaint persons responsible for the operation of elementary, secondary, and postsecondary schools with information about exemplary education programs, products, practices, and services; (2) assist such persons in implementing programs, products, and practices which such persons determine may improve the quality of education in the schools for which they are responsible, by providing materials, initial training, and ongoing implementation assistance; (3) ensure that all such activities, programs, products, and practices are subjected to rigorous evaluation with respect to their effectiveness and their capacity for implementation; (4) provide program development assistance toward the recognition, dissemination, and implementation of promising practices that hold the potential for answering critical needs and that have achieved credibility because of their effective use in schools; and (5) ensure that a substantial percentage of the innovations disseminated represent significant changes in practice for schools and teachers."

The sources listed in this section publish and/or distribute materials to help children with their mental health needs.

Active Parenting Publishers
810 Franklin Ct., Suite B
Marietta, GA 30067
(800) 825-0060
Distributes materials for parent education (for parents of children ages two through teenage), materials on loss education for preteens through adults, and self-esteem education for children ages 6-10.

A.D.D. WareHouse
300 NW 70th Ave.
Plantation, FL 33317
(800) 233-9273
Makes available Attention Deficit Disorder materials for educators to help students; programs to help parents and teachers build self-esteem; information on medication, behavior modification, and cognitive strategies for health care professionals; and books and videos for children and young teens.

AGS (American Guidance Service)
4201 Woodland Rd.
P.O. Box 99
Circle Pines, MN 55014-1796
(800) 328-2560
Distributes assessment and educational materials for clinical and classroom settings including tests and accessories for educational achievement/diagnosis, social skills development, and behavior assessment.

American Psychiatric Press, Inc.
1400 K Street NW
Washington, DC 20005
(800) 368-5777
(202) 789-2648 (Fax)
order@appi.org (e-mail)
http://www.appi.org (Internet)
Publishes materials for mental health professionals such as text books and reference guides on clinical treatments, practice management, practice guidelines, psychopharmacology, treatment of various mental disorders, and many more topics. Distributes *Issues in Mental Health,* a newsletter that lists textbooks and references on mental health issues including child and adolescent psychiatry.

Brunner/Mazel
19 Union Square West
New York, NY 10003
(212) 924-3344
Distributes books for professionals on a range of mental health topics addressing issues in childhood and adolescence.

Childswork/Childsplay
P. O. Box 61587
King of Prussia, PA 19406
(800) 962-1141
(610) 277-4556 (Fax)
http//childswork.com (Internet)
Distributes a wide array of products (books, therapeutic games, videotapes, computer software, etc.) for mental health professionals, school personnel, parents, and others who help children with the common and uncommon problems of childhood.

The Eating Disorders Bookshelf
Gurze Books
P.O. Box 2238
Carlsbad, CA 92018
(800) 756-7533
Provides a comprehensive free catalog listing more than 100 books on eating disorders.

Educators for Social Responsibility (ESR)
23 Garden St.
Cambridge, MA 02138
(800) 370-2515
(617) 864-5164 (Fax)
Distributes materials that teach "creative and productive ways to deal with differences, prevent violence, stimulate critical thinking about controversial issues, (and) promote cooperative problem solving" for early childhood and elementary students.

Families International Inc.
11700 W. Lake Park Dr.
Milwaukee, WI 53224
(414) 359-1040
(414) 359-1074 (Fax)
Distributes books, videos, and games for use by social workers and human service professionals on subjects such as anger, blended families, handling divorce, and effective stepparenting.

Product Sources

Free Spirit Publishing Inc.
400 First Ave., Suite 616
Minneapolis, MN 55401-1730
(800) 735-7323
help4kids@freespirit.com (e-mail)
Distributes books, posters, and other creative learning materials that deal with self-esteem, school success, creativity, healthy families, gifted education, learning differences, and humor.

The Guilford Press
72 Spring St.
New York, NY 10012
(800) 365-7006
(212) 966-6708 (Fax)
info@guilford.com (e-mail)
Publishes and distributes professional textbooks on topics including ADHD, anxiety, child abuse, childhood disorders, depression, eating disorders, sexual problems, and suicide from both behavioral and cognitive perspectives.

Institute for the Study of Children, Families & Communities
102 King Hall, Eastern Michigan University
Ypsilanti, MI 48197
(313) 487-0372
(313) 487-0284 (Fax)
Publishes and distributes over 20 workbooks and instructors manuals in its Foster Parent Education Series (some available in Spanish and French).

International Universities Press, Inc.
59 Boston Post Rd.
Box 1524
Madison, CT 06443-1524
(800) TELE-IUP
(203) 245-0775 (Fax)
Distributes books for professionals on a range of mental health topics including early childhood, adolescence, delinquency, and education.

Jason Aronson, Inc.
230 Livingston St.
Northvale, NJ 07647
(201) 767-4093
(201) 767-4330 (Fax)
http://www.aronson.com/ (Internet)

Publishes books for mental health professionals as well as *An Authoritative Guide to Books in Psychotherapy* that includes sections on abuse, adolescence, child therapy, child development, family therapy, and parenting.

Kidsrights
10100 Park Cedar Dr.
Charlotte, NC 28210
(800) 892-5437
Distributes books, videos, and other products on mental health subjects including family and self-esteem issues.

Menninger Video Productions
Altschul Group Corporation
1560 Sherman Ave., Suite 1000
Evanston, IL 60201
(800) 421-2363
(708) 328-6706 (Fax)

Mental Health Materials Center
P.O. Box 304
Bronxville, NY 10708
(914) 337-6596
Publishes and markets mental health educational materials for professionals and the public.

New Harbinger Self-Help Publications
5674 Shattuck Ave.
Oakland, CA 94609
(800) 748-6273
(510) 652-5472 (Fax)
newharbpub@aol.com (e-mail)
Publishes self-help texts and materials for a variety of issues and disorders.

PFLAG - Parents, Families and Friends of Lesbians and Gays
1101 14th St. NW, Suite 1030
Washington, DC 20005
(202) 638-4200
(202) 638-0243 (Fax)
pflagntl@aol.com (e-mail)
Publishes and distributes resources and publications on gay and lesbian issues and AIDS, with titles aimed at gay and lesbian youth, as well as books about gay and lesbian lifestyles for young readers.

Plenum Publishing Corp.
  233 Spring St.
  New York, NY 10013-1578
  (212) 620-8000
  (212) 463-0742 (Fax)
  books@plenum.com (e-mail)
  Professional books with an emphasis on developmental and cognitive psychology.

Psychological Corp.
  301 Commerce St., Suite 3700
  Fort Worth, TX 76102
  (817) 334-7500
  http://www.harcourtbrace.com/tpc-con.htm (Internet)
  Publishes and distributes materials pertaining to the mental health of children.

Sidran Foundation
  2328 W. Joppa Rd., Suite 15
  Lutherville, MD 21093
  (410) 825-8888
  sidran@access.digex.net (e-mail)
  Publishes books and educational materials on traumatic stress disorders, dissociative disorders, child sexual abuse, ritual abuse, self-injury, and self-help/recovery.

John Wiley & Sons, Inc.
  605 Third Ave.
  New York, NY 10158-0012
  (212) 850-6000
  (212) 850-6088 (Fax)
  Publishes and distributes professional textbooks, journals, software, etc. on child and adolescent psychology.

WPS (Western Psychological Services)
  12031 Wilshire Blvd.
  Los Angeles, CA 90025-1251
  (800) 648-8857
  (301) 478-7838 (Fax)
  Publishes and distributes assessment tools in the areas of clinical psychology, neuropsychology, school psychology, alcohol and drug abuse, special education, family counseling, and psychiatry.

Additional Directories on Children's Mental Health Services

Barton, H. et al. *The Directory of Model Programs to Prevent Mental Health Disorders*. Arlington, VA: National Mental Health Association, 1995.

Directory of National Helplines: A Guide to Toll-Free Helplines, Faxlines, Web Sites, and Other Public Service Numbers. Ann Arbor, MI: The Pierian Press, 1996.

Erickson, J. *Directory of American Youth Organizations*. Minneapolis: Free Spirit Publishing, 1996.

Mackenzie, L., Ed. *The Complete Directory for People with Learning Disabilities*. Lakeville, CT: Grey House Publishing, 1994.

Mackenzie, L., Ed. *The Complete Directory for People with Disabilities*. Lakeville, CT: Grey House Publishing, 1993.

Reed, M., Ed. *Healthcare Resource Directory*. Houston: Medical Productions, Inc., 1994.

White, B. & Madara, E., Eds. *The Self-Help Source Book*. Denville, NJ: American Self-Help Clearinghouse, 1995.

Witkin, M. et al. *Substance Abuse and Mental Health Services Administration (SAMHSA) Mental Health Directory*. Rockville, MD: U.S. Department of Health and Human Services, 1995.

Help Us Keep the Directory Up-to-Date

The Directory of Critical Information for Helping Children will be updated periodically. If you have information that should be included, and/or if you have found errors in this directory, please complete this form and mail it to: The Directory of Critical Information for Helping Children, The Center for Applied Psychology, P.O. Box 61587, King of Prussia, PA 19406 or fax it to (610) 277-4088.

Additional Information to be Added to the Directory:

NAME OF PROGRAM _____

ADDRESS _____

CITY/STATE/ZIP _____

PHONE (   ) _____

FAX (   ) _____

E-MAIL ADDRESS _____

WEB-SITE _____

CONTACT PERSON AND TITLE _____

PROGRAM DESCRIPTION _____

_____

_____

_____

TYPE OF ORGANIZATION _____

OTHER INFORMATION _____

_____

_____

Changes to be Made to the Directory:

PAGE # _____ CHANGES _____

_____

PAGE # _____ CHANGES _____

_____

PAGE # _____ CHANGES _____

_____

Your Name: _____

Address: _____

City/State/Zip _____

Phone (   ) _____

The Center for Applied Psychology, Inc. is the country's largest distributor of psychologically-oriented products, including therapeutic games, books, videotapes, audiotapes, computer software, posters, and teachers aids. Its *Childswork/Childsplay* catalog is designed to help professionals, parents, and teachers address the mental health needs of children and their families through play. Featuring over 100 resources that deal with such issues as impulsivity, divorce, self-control, coping skills, classroom behavior, family problems, bereavement, self-esteem, anger control and behavior problems, the product line has been lauded as the "most complete collection of products to help children with their social and emotional concerns."

The Center also provides up-to-date and innovative training in child and adolescent psychology for psychologists, social workers, and counselors throughout the year and throughout the U.S. Professionals can earn Continuing Education (CE) credits by attending workshops on such topics as Short-term Therapy with Children, Techniques and Strategies to Help the Angry Child, Adolescent Depression, Short-Term Therapy with Oppositional/Defiant Children, and Child Sexual Abuse.

The Childswork Book Club gives its members access to the most complete collection of psychotherapeutic books for children. Book Club members have the opportunity to purchase just-published and popular books on childhood concerns from ADHD to anger control, depression to divorce, and self-esteem to social skills. Featured titles as well as self-help books, therapeutic storybooks, and professional textbooks are offered at significant savings, as are other Childswork/Childsplay products.

The Child Therapy News is published bimonthly to offer mental health professionals the most complete source of information about a specific childhood disorder or issue. Each issue includes a full-length article detailing the most pertinent and up-to-date information of the subject, an in-depth interview with an expert, and a profile on a model treatment program. Past issues have addressed ADHD, anxiety disorders, sexual abuse, oppositional/defiant children, autism, gender identity disorders, child custody, and more.

For more information on the *Childswork/Childsplay* catalog, professional training, The Childswork Book Club, and/or *The Child Therapy News,* call 800/962-1141 or write The Center for Applied Psychology, Inc., P.O. Box 61587, King of Prussia, PA 19406.

A directory for adolescents and teens, *The Directory of Critical Information for Helping Adolescents,* is also available.

Notes

Notes

Notes

Notes

Notes

Notes

Notes